D1105635

"Lift High the Cross"

Executive Editor:
MSGR. THOMAS M. GINTY

General Editor:
MISS MARIA MEDINA

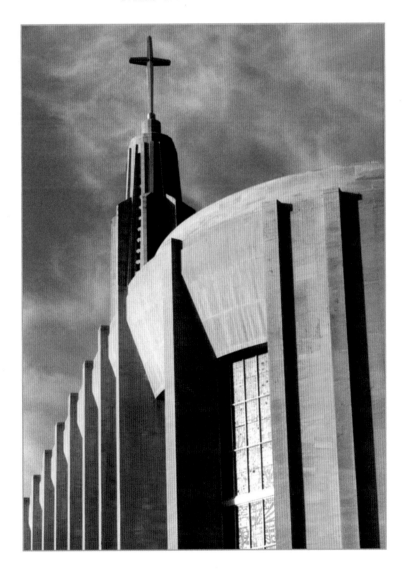

Contributing Authors:

MR. JOSEPH DUFFY   SR. DOLORES LIPTAK, RSM

ÉDITIONS
DU SIGNE

My dear friends in Christ,

Christianity finds its identity within the setting of this Sacred Story: that God so loved His people that He sent His Son to suffer on the cross, die, and rise triumphantly. In fact, the glorious hymn, "Lift High the Cross!" commemorates that story even as it has inspired generations of Christians to remember this startling reality. In particular, it reminds the local Church of Hartford that each generation has to proclaim the same message within its own particular corner of the Christian world.

This latest publication of the Archdiocese retraces the development of that very story within the Hartford setting. Based on the work of scholars who have recently written of the development of Hartford's Catholic community, this book provides a new venue for proclaiming the same message. In abbreviated prose as well as with well-chosen illustrations, it enables us to see, page by page, the graphic development of the Diocese, and later Archdiocese of Hartford, as it occurred during the exceptional leadership of its eleven Bishops. It shows how clergy, men and women religious, as well as committed laity took up the challenge of creating territorial and national parishes to serve the special needs of its membership. It makes clear that this was accomplished even while efforts were being made to build up structures to provide for the poor, the abandoned, the sick, and the uneducated.

The finger of God can clearly be seen as one traces the story of the continued sacrifice on the part of Hartford Catholics that made possible such growth and prominence. Out of the poverty through which it struggled in its first quarter century to the strong, respected place it holds today came a Church that can proudly take its place in proclaiming the Good News that God's Mercy can endure amidst both crisis and cooperative action. As these pages tell us, this, too, has been Hartford's story: Lift High the Cross!

I wish to thank those who contributed to the present volume, especially the editors, the archivist, the photographers, and those whose full-length works were reshaped to form the basis of the narrative. Their combined efforts demonstrate as clearly as the story itself that the present leadership and membership of the Church of Hartford reflect the selfless efforts that have been its constant story. Because of such shared commitment, the mission of the present Archdiocese of Hartford will continue to flourish.

With profound gratitude to God for His Divine Assistance in the past, and asking the continued outpouring of Divine Grace upon the Archdiocese of Hartford, I remain

Sincerely in Christ,

+ Daniel A. Cronin

Archbishop of Hartford

PREFACE

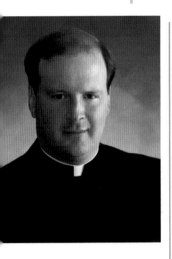

The recorded history of any diocese is often chronicled by a series of dates and events that have made a significant contribution to the founding and development of that diocese. They serve as a permanent record told in story fashion of the origins and rich history of each parish community. The objective of this particular fiftieth anniversary history of the Archdiocese of Hartford is not simply to record dates and view pictures, but to look into the very lives of the thousands of individuals who have sacrificed much to build the communities of faith that have formed and continue to enrich our two hundred eighteen parishes here in the Archdiocese of Hartford.

As you page through this work to learn of the rich history of the Archdiocese of Hartford, I hope that you will keep in mind that for the past one hundred and sixty years since the establishment of the Diocese of Hartford in 1843, the bishops, priests, deacons, men and women religious and dedicated lay individuals from many diverse ethnic traditions have called the Archdiocese of Hartford their home and have contributed much to the rich tapestry which is the Archdiocese of Hartford today. How unfortunate it would be if we viewed our history only in terms of important dates and prominent buildings. We believe our strength is measured in the willingness of each Roman Catholic to accept his/her baptismal promise to build up the body of Christ which is the Church.

As this work is being prepared for publication, I would like to thank, in a special way, Archbishop Daniel Cronin for commissioning this work and for his ongoing interest in this project. In addition, I would like to thank Sister Dolores Liptak, R.S.M., and Mr. Joseph Duffy for providing us with excerpts from their recent works on the history of the Archdiocese of Hartford. Sister Dolores' work entitled <u>Hartford's Catholic Legacy, Leadership</u> and Mr. Duffy's companion work entitled <u>Hartford's Catholic Legacy, Parishes</u> have been an invaluable assistance in the preparation of this anniversary book. I would also like to thank Father John Melnick and Miss Maria Medina for their time and patience in helping to select photos and to proofread the manuscript.

As we prepare to celebrate the fiftieth anniversary of the establishment of the Archdiocese of Hartford on August 6, 2003, may the many good works that have been accomplished in the past one hundred and sixty years continue to serve as a reminder to this generation and to generations yet to come of the value of being an active member of one's parish as we together "Lift High the Cross!".

Reverend Monsignor Thomas M. Ginty
Chancellor/Editor

Publisher:
EDITIONS DU SIGNE
B.P. 94 – 67038 Strasbourg, Cedex 2, France

Layout:
JULIETTE ROUSSEL

Photography:
PATRICE THÉBAULT
NANCY SCOTT

Publishing Director:
CHRISTIAN RIEHL

Director of Publication:
DR. CLAUDE –BERNARD COSTECALDE

Publishing Assistant:
JOËLLE BERNHARD

© Éditions du Signe, 2003
ISBN: 2-7468-0963-X
Printed in Italy by Arti Grafiche s.r.l. Pomezia (Rome)

INTRODUCTION

One can study the faces of the eleven Bishops who graced Connecticut Catholic history—one picture frame at a time. Their story appears as a series of tales that, in fact, reflects the experience of the entire family of God—clergy, lay, and religious. All trod the same path of solid service to the Church within the state's once Protestant, but now secular, Land of Steady Habits. Because these eleven were called to lead, the Church of Hartford developed its own unique charism.

Papal bull announcing the creation of the Diocese of Hartford, which included the States of Connecticut and Rhode Island, dated November 28, 1843.

Two patterns of episcopal leadership emerged during the tenure of the first two Bishops of Hartford. Both became the means by which the future of the Church was shaped. One aimed to reinforce the notion that Hartford's Catholic people, like those of every American religion, "belonged." Even Rome had understood the necessity of this strategy. As an ecumenical overture, officials of the Holy See had named the Reverend William Barber Tyler, a Protestant-American convert, as its first Bishop when the Diocese was established in 1843.

After his death, however, the second pattern of leadership became the norm for more than a century. It began with the administration of Hartford's second Bishop, Bernard O'Reilly. Since the Diocese had grown rapidly largely because of immigrants from the Emerald Isle, an Irish-immigrant perspective had taken hold. It strengthened under a succession of Irish-American prelates. Bishop O'Reilly and his successors tended to exhibit a more combative, defensive pattern of leadership. They preferred to protect and isolate Catholics because of their ethnic difference. When waves of newcomers came from Central, Eastern, and Southern Europe in the last decades of the nineteenth century, this second style was further reinforced. Guided by Irish-Americans, it created a European multi-ethnic fabric that characterized the Diocese of Hartford until the Second Vatican Council.

Letter dated November 26, 1843, appointing William Tyler as first Bishop of Hartford.

Cathedral of St. Joseph, Hartford taken by Fr. John McHugh during the installation ceremony for Archbishop Daniel A. Cronin January 28, 1992.

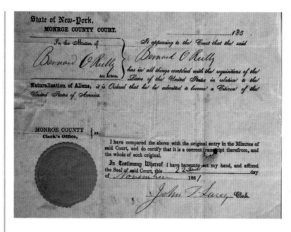

While each of Bishop O'Reilly's successors tended to follow his example of protecting ethnic minorities, they also saw themselves as following the pattern set by Bishop Tyler in every other regard. As stewards of God's grace, their first priority was always to supervise the spiritual and sacramental life of their people. Besides, they must search for clergy, invite women and men religious to become the educators and care providers for their people, found parishes, and build American Catholic institutions. These tasks alone were monumental.

BUILDING A NEW ENGLAND MISSION

The history of the Diocese of Hartford demonstrates the delicate balance that these competing needs presented as the Church evolved from mustard seed to evergreen. The seeds of the Church were planted in the Boston Church, first headed by the Bishop John Cheverus and his successor, Benedict J. Fenwick. In the initial decades of the 1800s, each took on the challenge of responding to the basic sacramental needs of the Catholics living outside the perimeters of Boston. In addition to caring for the Massachusetts Church, they located missionaries to serve the scattered Catholics in Connecticut and Rhode Island.

An issue of The Catholic Press, the first Catholic newspaper in Connecticut, begun in 1829.

The thriving city of Hartford became the original hub of Connecticut Catholic faith. There a small group of middle class converts wrote to Bishop Fenwick expressing not only the need for a resident priest but also a desire to begin a Catholic newspaper in order to combat anti-Catholicism. The Bishop viewed their request as a perfect proof of amazingly strong faith. With his permission, these businessmen launched the *Catholic Press*—only the second Catholic newspaper in the nation. Noting its success, Bishop Fenwick soon imitated the plan for the Boston Church; the paper he launched there survives today as the *[Boston] Pilot*.

TRINITY (CATHOLIC) CHURCH,
Talcott street, near Main.
The Church, of which the above is a representation, is

Drawing of the Most Holy Trinity Church, the first Catholic church in Connecticut, located in Hartford and precursor to St. Patrick-St. Anthony Church.

By 1829, Bishop Fenwick had come to realize that the desire of Connecticut's Catholic laity—businessmen and immigrant laborers—had to be addressed in a more consistent fashion. That year, he acceded to their joint request to establish a church and assign a resident pastor. The following year, a remodeled Protestant edifice, under the new title, Church of "the Holy and Undivided Trinity" was dedicated on the corner of Main and Talcott Streets—just a few blocks from the State House. With these bold moves, Catholic identity became a public reality. This action led, in 1843, to naming Hartford as the see city for all Catholics living south of Massachusetts.

ESTABLISHING A SOUTHERN NEW ENGLAND DIOCESE

First Bishop, William Tyler, brought to the Diocese a special Yankee perspective. His love for his adopted Roman Church was just as obvious. Greatly devoted to the Passion of Christ, he found comfort in serving the impoverished immigrants over whom he had assumed leadership. Most importantly, he strove to present the Catholic Church as both American and Roman Catholic. During the five years of his episcopacy, he looked for "good and holy" co-workers to sustain his aims. As he announced to the All Hallows, Dublin seminary rector: "It is not great learning but solid piety, a spirit of poverty and sincere zeal for the salvation of souls" that could "transform antagonistic Yankee attitudes."

By 1849, Bishop Tyler had fourteen priests to assist him and had founded a dozen parishes. Had consumption not taken his life at age forty-nine, he would probably have succeeded in convincing two congregations of women religious (the Sisters of Charity and the Sisters of Mercy) to share the same missionary challenge. Both Catholic and non-Catholic observers acknowledged his accomplishments. A *Providence Journal* obituary reported: "…To the portion of Protestants who enjoyed his friendship here, his name will [be] similar to those that attach to the memory of Cheverus." This was high praise, auguring well for the Diocese of Hartford.

After Bernard O'Reilly succeeded Bishop Tyler in 1850, this era of good feelings quickly abated. While aware of the aim of his predecessor to ease tensions, this second Bishop of Hartford also noted the growing tide of bigotry. The Church, he recognized, needed to defend itself, especially as floods of Irish immigrants began to threaten New England prejudice. His confrontative style proved disturbing to Protestants but not to beleaguered Catholics. The latter could count on their Bishop to respond to anti-Catholic vitriol with the pen and the spoken word. Even before coming to the Diocese, he had proven his ability to argue that Catholics must be granted the same freedoms that Protestants enjoyed. When he died only six years later, he had made it clear that the Catholic Church was a force to be noted.

In that short time, he had often defended his people; he also managed to establish sixty-three parishes or missions in Connecticut and seventeen more in Rhode Island. Besides, he had attracted many vocations. There were forty-one priests and twenty-two seminarians—mostly from Ireland—then at work in the Diocese. Furthermore, he had introduced the first group of women religious, the Sisters of Mercy, to care for orphans and the poor. If the French-Canadian or German clergy he tried to recruit had accepted his invitation, the Church of Hartford might have developed its reputation as a multi-ethnic institution even earlier. Unfortunately, this stalwart Bishop's varied attempts to protect and give pride to his people ended abruptly in 1856. The Collins steamship he boarded in Ireland after a recruitment trip foundered in the iceberg lanes of the North Atlantic. Bishop O'Reilly has the dubious honor of being the only American Bishop to die at sea.

During the episcopacy of American-born Francis Patrick McFarland, third Bishop of Hartford, a style that blended the irenic tones of Bishop Tyler with those of the defender, Bishop O'Reilly, began to develop. It eventually ushered in the style of leadership that was to typify Connecticut Catholicism for the next hundred years.

Bishop during the Civil War, Bishop McFarland noted how his people had moved from poverty to self-sufficiency as they labored in the state's booming war industries. As economic conditions improved, he became aware that the Diocese grew from a Church where being a Catholic required "a brave heart" to a Church that could graciously invite Catholics to settle in the state. Thus he sought every means to encourage the economic well-being as well as the spiritual improvement of his people.

To guide them spiritually, he recruited priests and, in fact, inspired so many recruits to the priesthood that it was reported, in 1868, that Hartford had the largest ordination class "ever held in the United States." He initiated a policy that sought clergy and brothers from other nations and acquired two orders of women religious—from Canada and the Low Countries—who began academies and parish schools. During his tenure, Hartford's immigrant Church took on more of the features of an American Church. Each succeeding Bishop came to understand that the Diocese would continue to prosper as long as immigrants could depend upon the Church to help them find acceptance in both Church and society.

CONCENTRATING ON THE CONNECTICUT CHURCH

In 1872, the jurisdictional boundaries that had combined the states of Connecticut and Rhode Island into one Diocese ended and Bishop McFarland returned the Episcopal residence to Hartford. Now Thomas Galberry, O.S.A., and Lawrence Stephen McMahon, whose tenure spanned the years 1878 until 1893, assumed the responsibility for helping immigrant Catholics develop within an American context.

Letter establishing the Diocese of Providence, 1872.

Both Bishops followed Bishop McFarland's policies. They shepherded the Diocese during the postwar period of rapid industrial expansion. Aware that Catholic newcomers belonged to the laboring classes, both Bishops made it clear that the rights of immigrants must be respected. Aligning themselves to the cause of American labor, the Bishops defended their struggles against the rich who "grow richer" while the poor became poorer. Both also sought ways to enhance Catholic pride, encouraging parishioners to build worthy churches and schools that would proclaim the greatness of their heritage in the midst of a Yankee world.

The Cathedral of SS. Peter and Paul, Providence, Rhode Island, seat of the Diocese of Hartford until 1872.

For this reason, both Bishops insisted upon the completion of Hartford's first Cathedral of St. Joseph. Bishop Galberry managed to dedicate the basement church on Farmington Avenue before his sudden death in 1878. Bishop McMahon had the honor of seeing to its completion. Because "…it was out of the offering of the poor and not out of the largess of the wealthy that …the finest church edifice in New England, was built," the new Cathedral proved a fitting example of what Catholics could accomplish. Debt-free at the time of its dedication in 1892, this Gothic masterpiece—the work of the renowned Patrick C. Keely—spoke through his architectural genius of a Church that was ready to take its place in Connecticut society.

Under both Bishops, furthermore, seminarians, congregations of women religious, and Catholic population multiplied rapidly. Bishop McMahon was the first, however, to recognize that a "perpetual Pentecost" had dawned upon the Diocese. Himself an immigrant, he wanted to protect newcomers by finding clergy and establishing parishes for any group that sought membership in the Hartford Church. He sought foreign-language speaking clergy to become pastors in his Diocese. Not only was he able to incardinate immigrant priests but he was also the first American Bishop to invite the French-based La Salette Fathers to re-establish their congregation in the United States. Moreover, he encouraged the newly-organized Scalabrinian Fathers of Piacenza, Italy to found parishes for Italian immigrants in New Haven. At the same time, when Slovak, Polish, and French-Canadian congregations organized mutual aid societies and sought permission to build churches in Bridgeport, Meriden, and several small towns in eastern Connecticut, Bishop McMahon worked with immigrant leaders to form parishes where their language and faith could be protected.

The original Cathedral of St. Joseph, designed by famed architect Patrick C. Keely and consecrated in 1892.

Other paramount concerns of Bishops Galberry and McMahon involved the education and health care of all Catholics. During the thirty months that he headed the Diocese, Bishop Galberry approved the establishment of the first "graded" parish schools and academies. He also sought to improve the intellectual life of adult Catholics by encouraging several Catholic laymen to begin the Hartford-based *Connecticut Catholic*, a paper that continues to this day under the title, *The Catholic Transcript*. This publication appealed primarily to second generation Irish-American Catholics. For this reason, Bishop McMahon sought alternative ways to see to it that the newest Polish, Slovak, French-Canadian and Italian Catholics were provided with ways to receive religious education and spiritual care. In particular, he approved the establishment of ethnic cultural societies.

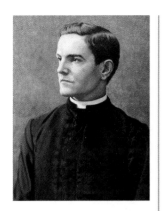

Rev. Michael J. McGivney, founder of the Knights of Columbus.

During Bishop McMahon's administration as well, the coordination of various institutions and lay ministries commenced. Thus, the Reverend John Russell was asked to supervise schools. Other clergy were named to take charge of societies affiliated with parishes. Expressing concern over the rise of fraternal organizations beyond parish boundaries, Bishop McMahon nevertheless decided to give official support, in 1882, to the New Haven-based Knights of Columbus, naming the Reverend Michael J. McGivney as first chaplain. This launched the now world-famous organization. All of these measures helped ease the way of immigrants into full participication in both Church and society.

FACING THE IMPLICATIONS OF EUROPEAN IMMIGRATION

The immigrant character of the Connecticut Catholic Church would become the major challenge of the Diocese's next two Bishops, Michael A. Tierney and John J. Nilan. They served the Church of Connecticut from 1894 until 1934. Both understood the immensity of the task of seeing to it that first- and second-generation immigrant Catholics find belonging. Particular credit must be given to Bishop Tierney for developing specific strategies for providing the means of this incorporation. Perhaps more so than any other American Bishop, in fact, he found ways to respond to the needs of European and Canadian immigrants to become incorporated into the U.S. Catholic Church.

Under Bishop Tierney, every minority group received special consideration. The result of this attention is the rich ethnic kaleidoscope that continues to define the Connecticut Church to this day. By the end of his term in 1908, almost one-half of the parishes inaugurated (37 of 71) had been organized just to serve newcomers from Central, Southern, and Eastern Europe. To further ensure that immigrants would continue to be cared for, Bishop Tierney looked for ways to make immigrants feel at home. Besides participating in national parish events, attending celebrations and visiting parishes, he initiated unique ways of finding new candidates to serve in national parishes. He encouraged clergy to come to the United States. He even traveled abroad, especially to Poland, to locate seminaries to prepare priests or missionaries willing to follow their people to the New World.

In addition, Bishop Tierney began the process of raising the consciousness of the more established Catholics of his Diocese to the needs of immigrants. He established St. Thomas, a minor seminary, to emphasize language and culture. He sent many of his students to complete their theological studies in seminaries

The original St. Thomas Seminary was located on Collins Street in Hartford.

from Belgium to the Austro-Hungarian and Russian Empires. He even sent some men to a Polish seminary in Detroit. In the meantime, he convinced two congregations, the Polish Vincentians and Franciscans, to send missionaries. Bishop Nilan did not deviate from the course begun by Bishop Tierney. Under him, national parishes were established, while additional clergy and congregations of women religious were recruited. He was even able to prepare second-generation Connecticut ethnic priests to become pastors in newly established national parishes.

While recognizing the significance of this challenge, Bishops Tierney and Nilan worked to maintain the steady growth of the Church of Connecticut within the context of American society. This required a careful monitoring of the continuing educational and health care needs of their people.

The present St. Thomas Seminary, whose cornerstone was laid in September 1928 in Bloomfield.

Parochial schools were added but attending public schools was also encouraged. Many of the new Catholic schools were put in charge of congregations that had been recruited to assume duties in the Diocese. Furthermore, adult education remained a priority. To ensure the religious character and intellectual caliber of *The Catholic Transcript*, Bishop Tierney named it the official paper of the Diocese. Reverend Thomas S. Duggan became its first priest-editor; he continued in that capacity during the Nilan years. In addition, a Diocesan Board of Education was created. Especially after 1910, Bishop Nilan developed the structure of Diocesan schools and saw to it that several junior-high and high schools were opened.

Health care first received special attention during Bishop Tierney's tenure. Aware that no previous Bishop had established a Catholic hospital, he founded five hospitals. Nursing communities of women were recruited to assume charge of these facilities. The first Catholic hospital in the diocese, St. Francis, located in Hartford, was founded and developed by Mother Ann Valencia and the Sisters of St. Joseph. In addition to the support given the original home for the elderly (St. Mary Home, West Hartford), he encouraged the beginnings of other

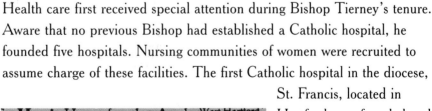

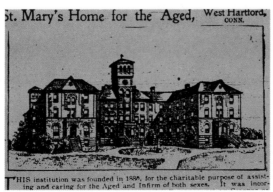

St. Mary's Home for the Aged, West Hartford, CONN.

THIS institution was founded in 1880, for the charitable purpose of assisting and caring for the Aged and Infirm of both sexes. It was incor-

Mother Ann Valencia, CSJ, foundress of St. Francis Hospital, Hartford.

nursing homes. Hartford's House of the Good Shepherd and St. John's, Deep River—both facilities for troubled youth—were begun during his administration. Bishop Nilan added just one additional major health care facility. In 1914, he officially opened St. Agnes Home, a West Hartford facility for unwed mothers and their babies.

Bishop Nilan's organizational skills also contributed greatly to the development of health and education facilities. Concerned that the various Catholic charities of the Diocese were not being properly coordinated, he established a Diocesan Bureau of Social Service. It coordinated the offices of Catholic Charities in the major cities of the state. Linked to these offices were national organizations, including associations known as the National Council of Catholic Women and of Men. During the first years of these various programs, schools of social services, mostly headed by, and attended by, lay women were conducted in the Diocese. This was in direct response to the call of Pope Pius XI that the laity be part of the call for Catholic Action.

Sr. Mary Rosa McDonough, RSM, first Dean of St. Joseph College, West Hartford.

Catholic Colleges in the Archdiocese include Albertus Magnus College , New Haven (left) and St. Joseph College, West Hartford (right).

In addition, Bishop Nilan recognized that the time had come to regularize programs for the Sister-teachers in his Diocese. He began the first normal schools to prepare the two largest congregations for teaching. He also responded positively to the request of both the Dominican Sisters of Ohio and the Sisters of Mercy to initiate collegiate programs for lay women of the Diocese. Albertus Magnus, New Haven, administered by the Dominicans, opened in 1925; St. Joseph College, West Hartford, run by the Sisters of Mercy, began in 1932.

*Three of the five hospitals
founded during
the episcopate of Bishop
Michael Tierney:
Raphael Hospital, New Haven,
St. Francis Hospital, Hartford,
Mary's Hospital, Waterbury.*

RESPONDING TO TWENTIETH CENTURY CHALLENGES

The Great Depression, the Second World War, the threat of Communism, and, finally, the dramatic sessions of the Second Vatican Council provided the Connecticut Catholic Church with far different challenges than had surrounded it during the years of incorporating immigrant Catholics. With the Depression, Catholics finally found common cause with their fellow Americans in matters of social consequence. Once the United States entered World War II, adherence to any religion became another uniting force that emphasized American loyalties. Finally, as the Council created dynamic change and worldwide attention, the Hartford Church found still other ways to clarify its role in an ecumenical and interfaith society. Maurice F. McAuliffe and Henry J. O'Brien, themselves natives to the state and former administrators of the seminary, were the Bishops charged with the responsibility of recognizing the unique opportunities made available by these unprecedented events.

Both addressed the often-conflicting social, political, and religious turn of events. During the Depression and World War, each searched for points of agreement with fellow citizens and joined in public debates when it was necessary to defend Church doctrine on social issues. Wherever possible, they sought ways to move the Catholic agenda into the mainstream. The measured approach of clergy and lay spokespersons appointed by them helped Catholics find their own voice. Since the Council called for more dramatic change within the structures of the Church itself, Bishop O'Brien guided the revolutionary approach to change.

World War II Chaplain's kit.

The Connecticut Church grew stronger as it successfully managed every one of the transforming events of the twentieth century. During the war, for example, urban parishes recovered from Depression woes and new parishes were established expressly to serve war workers. Catechetical programs and centers were begun for workers lured to war-related employment throughout the state. Women religious began child-care facilities for mothers employed in war-related industries, especially in the key cities. Fifty-five priests volunteered for service. Chaplain Neil J. Doyle, a victim of wounds incurred near the Solomon Islands, was the only priest to die but others faced constant danger in the European theater—some landing with troops on D-Day—or serving aboard ships in the Pacific. Nurse-graduates of the state's Catholic hospitals spent years in overseas duty.

In the post-war period, Diocesan expansion continued at full pace. By 1953, the Church comprised some 750,000 Catholics of some 1,900,000 inhabitants and was considered "one of the most solidly established and best managed dioceses in the nation." By then it was clear that the number of parishes, as well as the increase of Catholic population, warranted the restructuring of diocesan jurisdictions. Heading the Diocese since 1945, Bishop O'Brien presided over the separation of the Diocese into three divisions in 1953. The Archdiocese of Hartford, including the three counties of Hartford, New Haven, and Litchfield, assumed the role of Metropolitan See. This newly configured Hartford Church remained rich in Catholic population, had more than 400 priests, and some 30 congregations of women religious to provide direct services.

Letter and poem from "a friend" sent to The Catholic Transcript commemorating the life of Rev. Neil J. Doyle, the only priest casualty for the Diocese of Hartford during World War II

Papal bull creating the Diocese of Norwich and the Diocese of Bridgeport, splitting the state of Connecticut into three dioceses, dated August 1953. Hartford would become an archdiocese.

BEGINNING THE ARCHDIOCESE OF HARTFORD

Henry J. O'Brien presided as the first Archbishop of Hartford until 1968. As was true of the first Bishop of Hartford, he faced all the challenges that the reorganization requires. An unexpected crisis was the tragic loss of the Cathedral, destroyed by fire one wintry night in December, 1956. No sooner had the monumental task of rebuilding been completed when Archbishop O'Brien was called upon to respond to the second challenge—that of presiding over the transitions following the Second Vatican Council. If the Archbishop had watched "his cathedral die," he was now called upon, both figuratively and literally, to supervise a new Church rising.

The original Cathedral of St. Joseph, which was destroyed by fire on December 31, 1956.

Cathedral Building Fund campaign booklet.

Current Cathedral of St. Joseph, consecrated in 1962.

Left: News conference held on November 20, 1968 Archbishop Henry J. O'Brien announcing his retirement.

Right: Then Auxiliary Bishop of Cleveland John F. Whealon greeting Pope Paul VI at the Second Vatican Council.

Helen Margaret Feeney, C.S.J. Chancellor (1986-1994)

Despite the fact that clergy, religious, and laity provided steadiness and became supportive instruments of the changing times, the burden of that transition wore heavily upon Archbishop O'Brien. Still, he provided excellent direction to clergy and laity. He saw the changes as reflecting the mentality of Catholic Action. His advise was simple; the work of lay ministry was "not only [one] in which the people help the priest do the priest's work. ….[In the real lay apostolate, the priest helps the layman do the layman's work." An American Church, following the directives of the Vatican Council, developed in the midst of this perspective. Weakened by ill health, the Archbishop was forced to resign in 1968.

Because John F. Whealon, who assumed office in 1969, had participated in the deliberations of Vatican II, Connecticut Catholics were reassured that the reforms of the Council would be fulfilled. They were not to be disappointed. Under his direction, the Hartford Church found innovative ways to approach the post-Vatican II world. In Archbishop Whealon's own words, he was *Vox Clamantis in Deserto*. This perspective was most evident in the Archbishop's continued efforts to appoint lay men and women, as well as women religious, to head key chancery and tribunal positions. In addition, he developed a permanent deaconate program surpassed only by the Archdiocese of Chicago. When he died suddenly in 1991, almost twenty-four years after his ordination as Archbishop, dozens of offices and organizations, run largely by laity, supported the Archdiocese in many of its new ministries and organizations.

Front page of the August 9, 1991 edition of The Catholic Transcript announcing the sudden death of Archbishop John F. Whealon.

Archbishop Daniel A. Cronin at the groundbreaking of St. Bridget School, Cheshire, March 3,1998.

RESPONDING TO ONE HUNDRED FIFTY YEARS

This was the Archdiocese inherited by Archbishop Daniel A. Cronin in 1992. Installed as eleventh Bishop and third Archbishop of Hartford, he directs a Catholic people who remain hardworking, unobtrusive, sharply focused on social issues, and extremely well educated. Archbishop Cronin's desire was to tap the rich resources his membership possessed so that, together, they could "Lift High The Cross." A New Englander himself who had returned from Vatican assignments to head the Church of Fall River in 1970, Archbishop Cronin accepted this challenge with quiet joy. Here was a Diocese whose members had responded appropriately to every crisis that had confronted them. He reminded the Hartford Catholic community that his own task was equally simple. After all, so much had already been accomplished by the "priests, deacons, religious and laity of the Diocese." He expected to "build upon [these] wonderful accomplishments." Like John Paul II, his words and actions insisted: "Be Not Afraid." Ten years into his tenure, Connecticut Catholics can also look at all that has been done with gratitude and anticipate *ad multos annos*.

Sister Dolores Liptak, RSM
Sisters of Mercy Administrative Offices,
West Hartford, Connecticut
July, 2002

[Sister Dolores is an educator and author. Two of her books, *European Immigrants and the Catholic Church in Connecticut* and *Hartford's Catholic Legacy: Leadership*, form the basis for this brief overview.]

ARCHDIOCESE OF HARTFORD

BISHOPS & ARCHBISHOPS, 1844 – PRESENT

Bishop William Tyler

1844-1849

Spes Nostra

BORN JUNE 5, 1806
IN DERBY, VERMONT
ORDAINED JUNE 3, 1829
CONSECRATED BISHOP OF HARTFORD MARCH 17, 1844
DIED JUNE 18, 1849

Bishop Bernard O'Reilly

1850-1856

Spes Nostra

BORN MARCH 1, 1803
IN CUNNAREEN, COUNTY LONGFORD, IRELAND
ORDAINED OCTOBER 15, 1831
CONSECRATED BISHOP OF HARTFORD NOVEMBER 10, 1850
PERISHED AT SEA JANUARY 1856

Bishop Francis P. McFarland

1858-1874

Spes Nostra

BORN APRIL 4, 1819
IN WAYNESBORO, PENNSYLVANIA
ORDAINED MAY 18, 1845
CONSECRATED BISHOP OF HARTFORD MARCH 14, 1858
DIED OCTOBER 12, 1874

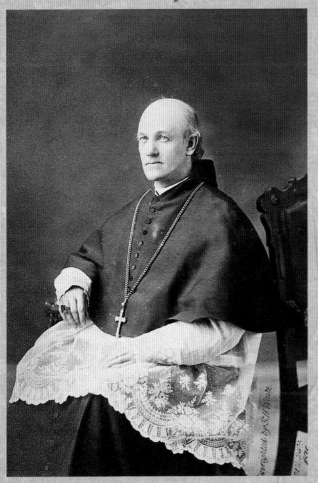

Bishop Thomas Galberry, O.S.A.

1876-1878

Spes Nostra

BORN MAY 28, 1833
IN NAAS, COUNTY KILDARE, IRELAND
ORDAINED DECEMBER 20, 1856
CONSECRATED BISHOP OF HARTFORD MARCH 19, 1876
DIED OCTOBER 10, 1878

Bishop Lawrence S. McMahon

1879-1893

Spes Nostra

BORN DECEMBER 26, 1835
IN ST. JOHN, BRUNSWICK, CANADA
ORDAINED MARCH 24, 1860
CONSECRATED BISHOP OF HARTFORD AUGUST 10, 1879
DIED AUGUST 21, 1893

Bishop Michael Tierney

1894-1908

Spes Nostra

BORN SEPTEMBER 29, 1839
IN BALLYLOOBY, COUNTY TIPPERARY, IRELAND
ORDAINED MAY 26, 1866
CONSECRATED BISHOP OF HARTFORD FEBRUARY 22, 1894
DIED OCTOBER 5, 1908

Bishop John Joseph Nilan

1910-1934

Dominus Firmamentum Meum

BORN AUGUST 1, 1855
IN NEWBURYPORT, MASSACHUSETTS
ORDAINED DECEMBER 2, 1878
CONSECRATED BISHOP OF HARTFORD APRIL 28, 1910
DIED APRIL 13, 1934

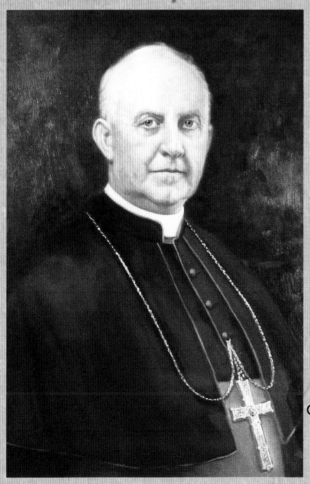

Bishop Maurice F. McAuliffe

1934-1944

In Caritate Dei

BORN JUNE 17, 1875
IN HARTFORD, CONNECTICUT
ORDAINED JULY 29, 1900
CONSECRATED AUXILIARY BISHOP OF HARTFORD APRIL 28, 1926
APPOINTED BISHOP OF HARTFORD APRIL 25, 1934
DIED DECEMBER 15, 1944

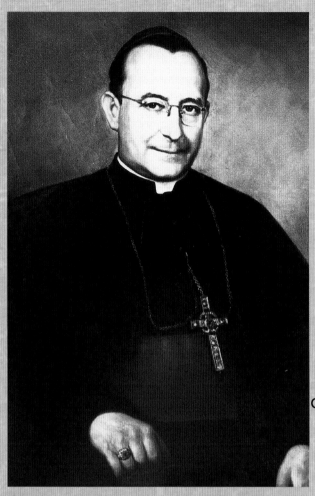

Archbishop Henry J. O'Brien

1945-1968

Christus Crescat

Archbishop John F. Whealon

1969-1991

Vox Clamantis In Deserto

Archbishop Daniel A. Cronin

1992-present

Ad Oboediendum Fidei

BORN NOVEMBER 14, 1927
IN NEWTON, MASSACHUSSETTS
ORDAINED DECEMBER 20, 1952
APPOINTED AUXILIARY BISHOP OF BOSTON JUNE 10, 1968
APPOINTED BISHOP OF FALL RIVER OCTOBER 30, 1970
APPOINTED ARCHBISHOP OF HARTFORD DECEMBER 10, 1991
INSTALLED ARCHBISHOP OF HARTFORD JANUARY 28, 1992

ARCHBISHOPS

Bishop John Gregory Murray

1920 – 1925

Mea Omnia Tua

BORN FEBRUARY 26, 1877 IN WATERBURY, CONNECTICUT
ORDAINED APRIL 14, 1900
CONSECRATED AUXILIARY BISHOP OF HARTFORD APRIL 28, 1920
APPOINTED BISHOP OF PORTLAND, MAINE OCTOBER 12, 1925
APPOINTED ARCHBISHOP OF ST. PAUL, MINNESOTA JANUARY 25, 1932
DIED OCTOBER 10, 1956

Bishop Maurice F. McAuliffe

1925 – 1934

In Caritate Dei

BORN JUNE 17, 1875 IN HARTFORD, CONNECTICUT
ORDAINED JULY 29, 1900
APPOINTED AUXILIARY BISHOP OF HARTFORD DECEMBER 17, 1925
CONSECRATED AUXILIARY BISHOP OF HARTFORD APRIL 28, 1926
APPOINTED BISHOP OF HARTFORD APRIL 25, 1934
DIED DECEMBER 15, 1944

Bishop Henry J. O'Brien

1940 – 1945

Christus Crescat

BORN JULY 21, 1896 IN NEW HAVEN, CONNECTICUT
ORDAINED JULY 8, 1923
CONSECRATED AUXILIARY BISHOP OF HARTFORD MAY 14, 1940
APPOINTED NINTH BISHOP OF HARTFORD APRIL 7, 1945
APPOINTED ARCHBISHOP OF HARTFORD AUGUST 6, 1953
RESIGNED 1968
DIED JULY 23, 1976

Bishop John F. Hackett

1952– 1986

Manete in Christo

BORN DECEMBER 7, 1911 IN NEW HAVEN, CONNECTICUT
ORDAINED JUNE 29, 1936
APPOINTED AUXILIARY BISHOP OF HARTFORD DECEMBER 10, 1952
ORDAINED AUXILIARY BISHOP OF HARTFORD MARCH 19, 1953
RETIRED DECEMBER 7, 1986
DIED MAY 30, 1990

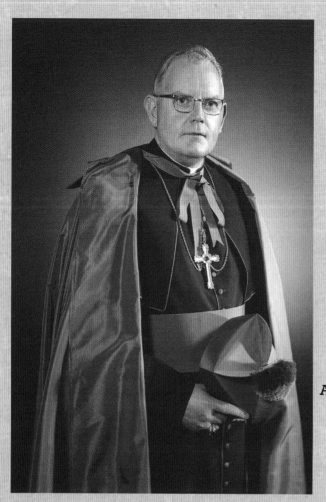

Bishop Joseph F. Donnelly

1964 – 1977

Opus Justitiae Pax

BORN MAY 1, 1909 IN NORWICH, CONNECTICUT
ORDAINED JUNE 29, 1934
APPOINTED AUXILIARY BISHOP OF HARTFORD NOVEMBER 9, 1964
DIED JUNE 30, 1977

Bishop Peter A. Rosazza

1978-present

Adveniat Regnum Tuum

BORN FEBRUARY 13, 1935 IN NEW HAVEN, CONNECTICUT
ORDAINED JUNE 29, 1961
APPOINTED AUXILIARY BISHOP OF HARTFORD FEBRUARY 28, 1978
ORDAINED AUXILIARY BISHOP OF HARTFORD JUNE 24, 1978

Bishop Paul S. Loverde

1988 – 1994

Encourage and Teach
with Patience

Born September 3, 1940 in Framingham, Massachusetts
Ordained December 18, 1965
Appointed Auxiliary Bishop of Hartford February 3, 1988
Ordained Auxiliary Bishop of Hartford April 12, 1988
Installed as Bishop of Ogdensburg January 17, 1994
Installed as Bishop of Arlington March 25, 1999

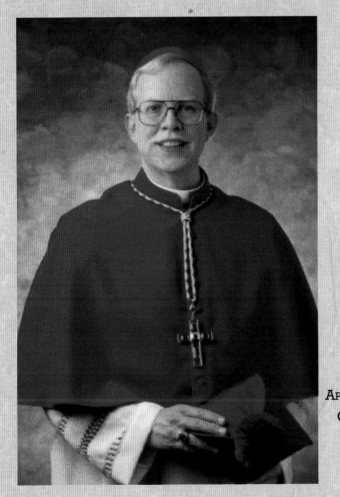

Bishop Christie A. Macaluso

1997 – Present

Veritas Liberabit Vos

Born June 12, 1945 in Hartford, Connecticut
Ordained May 22, 1971
Appointed Auxiliary Bishop of Hartford March 18, 1997
Ordained Auxiliary Bishop of Hartford June 10, 1997

ARCHDIOCESE OF HARTFORD, CONNECTICUT

BRANCHES...
PARISHES AND MISSIONS

*"But when it has grown,
it is the biggest of shrubs.
It becomes a tree
so that the bird of the air can come
and shelter in its branches!"*

ASSUMPTION, ANSONIA

Established 1870
Current Co-Pastors: Fathers George P. Burnett and Robert F. Condron
More than 1200 households

Ansonia's Irish Catholics became the pastoral responsibility of Derby (then Birmingham). In 1853, a Catholic School opened on Main Street and continued for about seven years. Under the direction of Father Patrick J. O'Dwyer of Derby, a frame church was erected on Main and Green Streets. Bishop Francis P. McFarland dedicated the chapel on August 23, 1868. Father O'Dwyer became Ansonia's first resident pastor on June 20, 1870, as parish status was conferred on the mission. The third pastor, Father Joseph Synnott, contracted the services of well-known church architect Patrick C. Keely to design a new church. On June 17, 1900, Bishop Michael A. Tierney blessed Assumption's basement chapel of the Sacred Heart and later dedicated the completed church on June 23, 1907.

Two years after that a parochial school was built and dedicated on August 21, 1910.

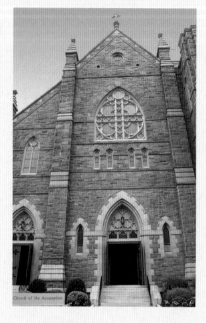

Church of the Assumption

HOLY ROSARY, ANSONIA

Italian
Established 1908
Current Pastor: Father Ronald L. Genua
More than 700 households

Bishop John J. Nilan created Holy Rosary parish for Ansonia's Italian immigrants in 1908. The appointed pastor was Father Francis Bonforti, who celebrated the first parish Mass on October 4, 1908. Italian Catholics were worshipping at the former Assumption Parish Church on Main Street, a Gothic brick edifice whose cornerstone was blessed on August 15, 1867. This old church was renamed Holy Rosary. Because the congregation continued to grow, the fourth pastor, Father Vincent Iannetta, implemented a construction program. Archbishop Henry J. O'Brien dedicated the new Holy Rosary Church in 1967.

ST. ANTHONY, ANSONIA

Lithuanian
Established 1915
Current Administrator: Father Patrick J. Berkery
Nearly 200 households

Father Joseph Zebris of Waterbury celebrated Mass periodically for Ansonia's Lithuanian colony in the mid-1890s. A sufficient number of Lithuanians was present by 1896 to establish a chapter of the Lithuanian Alliance. By 1907 members incorporated their society with the purpose of founding their own church. Bishop John J. Nilan, however, rebuffed the Lithuanian delegation in their desire for a separate ethnic parish, preferring that the immigrants remain within Assumption parish. In 1912, they proceeded to build a church without episcopal approval, hoping that Bishop Nilan would accede to their wishes. The Bishop maintained his previous stance that Assumption should serve the Lithuanians. With the aid of a local Byzantine priest, Ansonia's Lithuanians appealed successfully to Rome in the fall of 1915. As a direct result, Bishop Nilan was ordered to allow a Lithuanian parish of St. Anthony to operate independently. On Thanksgiving Day 1915, Father Matthew Pankus of Bridgeport dedicated the church. Father Vincent Bukavecias was named first pastor.

ST. JOSEPH, ANSONIA

Polish
Established 1925
Current Pastor: Father Marek W. Sobczak, C.M.
Parochial Vicar: Father Joseph Szpilski, C.M.
More than 400 households

Before 1905, Polish immigrants attended Ansonia's Assumption parish. When St. Michael Polish parish was established in Derby on October 14, 1905, Ansonia's Polish Catholics traveled there instead. St. Michael pastor, Father Joseph Studzinski, bought a parcel of land on Jewett Street, Ansonia, for a future church. In June 1925, Bishop John J. Nilan appointed Vincentian Father Aloysius Zielenznik, C.M., as pastor of the new St. Joseph parish. The priest's first Mass for the Polish congregation was celebrated on July 12, 1925, at a Central Street hall rented from an Italian society. With remarkable speed, a self-contained parish plant was constructed and was soon in operation, with church, school, and convent all compacted into a rectangular brick building. The church was dedicated on September 6, 1926. Ten days later, St. Joseph school opened, staffed by the Sisters of the Holy Family of Nazareth.

ST. ANN, AVON

Established 1917
Current Pastor: Father Thomas E. McCarthy
Parochial Vicar: Father Vittorio Guerrera
1900 households

Famed New Britain pastor Father Luke Daly, who worked throughout the Farmington Valley, probably visited Avon around 1848. By 1869, circuit pastors from Collinsville were offering home Masses every three months. The founding families of Avon Catholicism were Irish, but soon Polish and Italian immigrants came, seeking employment at Ensign-Bickford and the Alsop farm. With the growing Catholic ranks, Father William P. Kennedy of Collinsville began to celebrate liturgies at Towpath School in 1917. Two years later, on December 17, a frame chapel on Mountain View Avenue was dedicated to St. Ann. In 1922, St. Ann became a mission of St. Patrick in Farmington. Finally, on May 20, 1944, St. Ann was made a parish, with Father John T. Hynes appointed first resident pastor. In August 1955, Father William J. Gerrity purchased nearly nine acres of land at the intersection of West Avon and Arch Roads

for a new church. Archbishop Henry J. O'Brien dedicated the new St. Ann church and rectory on June 1, 1957.

OUR LADY OF GRACE, BANTAM

Established 1970
Current Pastor: Father John McCann, S.M.M.
Nearly 300 households

During World War II, Father James F. Egan, pastor of St. Anthony, Litchfield, offered Mass for Bantam Catholics at the Community Center. Catholics of Bantam had already been raising money for their own church. In July 1949, ground was broken on Route 202 for Our Lady of Grace mission chapel. Father Egan celebrated the first mission Mass in the new frame edifice on December 18, 1949. In 1970, Our Lady of Grace was

made a parish by Archbishop John J. Whealon. Father Stanley A. Kwasnik was designated first resident pastor and celebrated the first parish liturgy for families drawn from Bantam, New Preston and Morris on June 16.

St. Michael, Beacon Falls

Established 1899
Current Pastor: Father Leonard J. Kvedas
About 800 households

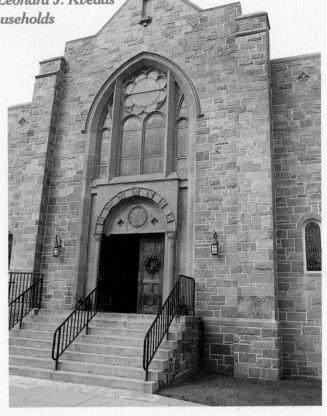

In 1885, Beacon Falls became a mission of St. Augustine, Seymour, under Father Richard Gragan. Mass was offered at first in a Main Street home and later at Clark's Hall and Brown's Hall. By the turn of the century, Beacon Falls Catholics raised funds for their own church, which was erected at the corner of Church and Main Streets. Father Michael Rigney celebrated the first Mass there on Christmas Day. Bishop Michael A. Tierney dedicated St. Michael Church on March 11, 1900. Bishop John J. Nilan elevated St. Michael to a parish on November 15, 1924, naming Father Jeremiah J. McAuliffe as first resident pastor. At this time, neighboring Oxford had become a mission of Beacon Falls. Under the fourth pastor, Father Jerome T. Cook, the church property was sold to the state of Connecticut for highway construction purposes. From 1941-42 liturgies were celebrated at a former theater. On October 12, 1941 Bishop Maurice F. McAuliffe blessed the cornerstone of the new St. Michael Church. Finally, Archbishop Henry J. O'Brien dedicated the church on June 24, 1956.

Church of the Nativity, Bethlehem

Established 1916
Current Pastor: Father Richard L. Shellman
More than 450 households

When St. John Church, Watertown, became a parish in 1884, Bethlehem was its mission. Anticipating an expansion of mission population, Father John J. Loftus purchased land in 1915 on East Street. A building on the parcel was refitted to serve as a mission church. In 1928, Watertown pastor Father Cornelius P. Teulings erected a Spanish-style church on the mission's East Street acreage. The edifice was joyfully dedicated in October 1929. Bethlehem remained a faithful mission of Watertown until 1972, when Father Carl J. Sherer was appointed resident pastor by Archbishop John F. Whealon. An ambitious building fund for a new church was launched in the early 1990's by then pastor Father Henry R. Dery. The modern church was built on Nativity's seven-acre East Street property and dedicated on October 11, 1992.

SACRED HEART, BLOOMFIELD

Established 1878
Current Pastor: Father Aidan N. Donahue
More than 800 households

In 1878, the first Mass in rustic Bloomfield, a land of tobacco and farms, was said by Father Joseph Reid of St. Joseph Cathedral, Hartford, of which Bloomfield was a mission. Father Reid was succeeded by Father William Harty who built a church on Woodland Avenue in 1878. Bishop Thomas Galberry blessed the cornerstone of Sacred Heart Mission, and later Bishop Lawrence S. McMahon dedicated the finished edifice. In 1881, Bloomfield became the mission of St. Bernard, Tariffville. At the turn of the century, Father John T. Downey of the newly created St. Michael parish in Hartford ministered to Bloomfield. In 1924 when Father Francis P. Nolan built St. Justin Church in Hartford, Sacred Heart became its mission. In 1934, Sacred Heart reverted again to the care of St. Thomas Seminary, Bloomfield. Finally, in 1947, Sacred Heart mission became a parish with Father Harold F. Daly as first resident pastor. Ground was broken on May 13, 1962, for a new church and school, staffed by the Sisters of Charity from Baltic. Sacred Heart Church and School was dedicated on April 27, 1963, by Archbishop Henry J. O'Brien. Unfortunately, the school was forced to close in June 1988, and the building was converted into a Family Life Center. In 1996, Christ the King Church, Bloomfield, merged with Sacred Heart.

ST. ELIZABETH, BRANFORD

Established 1966
Current Pastor: Father Ralph M. Colicchio
More than 700 households

St. Elizabeth, Branford, was established in June 1934 by Bishop Maurice F. McAuliffe as a mission under the care of St. Vincent de Paul Parish, East Haven. On August 18, the first mission Mass was celebrated in temporary quarters in a Bradley Street dance hall. In December 1935, a mission chapel at Short Beach was dedicated to St. Elizabeth. In 1947, St. Elizabeth passed to the care of the newly created St. Clare parish, East Haven. Despite rapid growth in the Short Beach area during the post-World War II years, parish status was not conferred until September 22, 1966. Father John F. Tierney was appointed first pastor of St. Elizabeth by Archbishop Henry J. O'Brien. Soon a splendid new church on Burban Drive replaced the old Short Beach Chapel, dedicated on December 7, 1969, by Archbishop John F. Whealon.

St. Mary of the Immaculate Conception, Branford

Established 1868
Current Pastor: Father Vincent A. Brown
Parochial Vicars: Fathers Robert F. Birmingham
and William Seery
More than 2500 households

In the summer of 1851, Father John Sheridan of St. Mary, New Haven, celebrated the first Branford Mass at the Montowese Street home of Francis Harding. In 1852 the area passed to the jurisdiction of the newly created St. Patrick parish, New Haven. In 1854 Branford passed to the care of St. Joseph, Chester. The first Branford mission chapel, dedicated to the Immaculate Conception, was completed in 1855 on land donated by Mr. Harding. In 1856 it became a dependency of Guilford. In October 1858, Father William Clarke was named first pastor of the newly created parish. Father Edward Martin organized a church building project. The completed church was dedicated by Bishop Michael Tierney on January 24, 1904. The parish church soon had to be rebuilt after a tragic fire on November 25,

1904. The church was rededicated a month later. By the early 1960's a new school, staffed by the Sisters of Notre Dame de Namur, was dedicated on June 3, 1961, by Archbishop Henry J. O'Brien. A second church fire of suspicious origin necessitated the replacement of the old church. The new St. Mary was dedicated on August 25, 1974, by Archbishop John F. Whealon.

St. Therese, Branford

Established 1947
Current Pastor: Father Raymond J. Barry
800 households

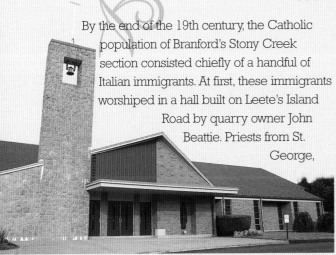

By the end of the 19th century, the Catholic population of Branford's Stony Creek section consisted chiefly of a handful of Italian immigrants. At first, these immigrants worshiped in a hall built on Leete's Island Road by quarry owner John Beattie. Priests from St. George,

Guilford, ministered to Stony Creek. A chapel on School Street eventually replaced the Beattie hall worship site and remained in use until 1927. Father John C. Fogarty of St. George then built a new church and rectory on Thimble Islands Road. Bishop John J. Nilan dedicated both in October 1928. On May 23, 1947, then Bishop Henry J. O'Brien made St. Therese mission a parish, which absorbed a parcel of territory from St. Mary parish that included the picturesque Thimble Islands. Father Francis Breen was appointed founding pastor. On August 31, 1968, the new St. Therese on Leete's Island Road was dedicated by Auxiliary Bishop John F. Hackett. In 1974, the old church on Thimble Islands Road was sold to the town.

St. Ann, Bristol

French
Established 1908
Current Pastor: Father Robert J. Rousseau
Almost 1400 households

During the late 19th century, waves of French Catholics migrated to Connecticut from Canada and Maine. With 200 French families in Bristol by 1905, three representatives met with Bishop Michael A. Tierney to request a separate parish for French-Canadians. As a result, Father Joseph P. Perreault was appointed first pastor on November 28 at the old Town Hall on Main Street. By January 1908, the liturgical celebrations were moved to the second floor of the J.H. Sessions and Son factory on North Main Street. A site for a parish church was selected in July at the corner of West and Gaylord Streets. A basement church was erected and hosted its first Mass on Christmas Day 1908. Father Perreault next planned a school and convent to fulfill the desires of his parishioners for a Catholic education for their children. St. Ann School opened on September 4, 1918, staffed by the Sisters of the Assumption of the Blessed Virgin Mary. On December 20, 1953, Archbishop Henry J. O'Brien dedicated a new St. Ann Church on top of the old basement church. In 1982 the Sisters of the Assumption departed, and the school became lay-staffed, eventually closing in June 1989.

St. Anthony, Bristol

Italian
Established 1920
Current Pastor: Father Nicholas P. Melo
1200 households

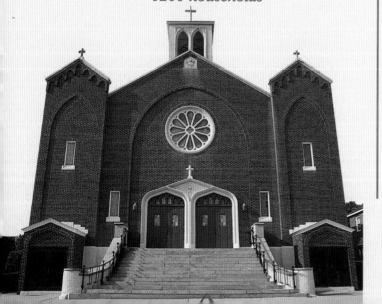

The first Italian immigrant family settled in Bristol about 1901, attending St. Joseph Church. By 1920, Italians were determined to have their own parish for a fuller ethnic expression of their spirituality. Bishop John J. Nilan appointed Father Luigi Becarris as founding pastor of the newly incorporated St. Anthony Parish in 1920. A church was quickly constructed, and Mass was first offered in the parish church on December 19, 1920. A larger church was soon required for the burgeoning congregation, and a new St. Anthony Church was dedicated on November 30, 1930. In 1939, third pastor Father Settimio Crudele opened St. Anthony Elementary School in the old church. Eleven years later, he added to his parish's educational system by opening St. Anthony High School in the renovated Veeder-Root factory. The high school closed in 1967.

ST. GREGORY THE GREAT, BRISTOL

Established 1957
Current Pastor: Father John J. Georgia
Parochial Vicar: Father Christopher P. Meade
About 2900 households

Father Charles W. McNerney was appointed founding pastor of St. Gregory the Great parish, Bristol, on November 21, 1957. Three days later, the first parish Mass was offered at the Stafford School. Parishioner Frank Janicke converted the temporary rectory's three-car garage on Farmington Avenue into a chapel for daily Mass. Through the kindness of town authorities, the Stafford School was employed for weekly religious instruction. By 1965, the facilities of the Northeast School were also in use. On November 5, 1960, Archbishop Henry J. O'Brien dedicated St. Gregory the Great Church on property adjoining the new rectory on Maltby Street.

ST. JOSEPH, BRISTOL

Established 1864
Current Pastor: Father James F. Leary
Parochial Vicar: Father Robert Villa
1250 households

Catholicism in Bristol originated in the 1840's with Irish immigrants who worked the copper mine between Bristol and Unionville. After mine workers went on strike because no time was permitted to attend Sunday Mass, Father Luke Daly of Hartford was invited to celebrate Mass around 1848. Later, Bristol became a mission of St. Mary's, New Britain. On July 12, 1854, the circuit pastor purchased the Titus Merriman property, the site of the present church. Construction of a frame church began in 1858 and it was dedicated to St. Joseph on August 26, 1860. On October 1, 1864, Father Michael B. Rodden was appointed resident pastor as St. Joseph mission was made a parish. Father Thomas Keena undertook the construction of a parochial school on the Queen Street tract, and the new school was dedicated on May 24, 1903, staffed by the Sisters of St. Joseph of Chambery. On the site of the first church Father Oliver T. Magnell undertook the building of a new one, which was dedicated on August 9, 1925. The original church was moved and eventually torn down to make way for the new. On November 13, 1960, the

contemporary school on Center Street was blessed. For the 125th anniversary of the parish, the interior of the church was completely renovated to bring the church into conformity with the liturgy as renewed by the Second Vatican Council.

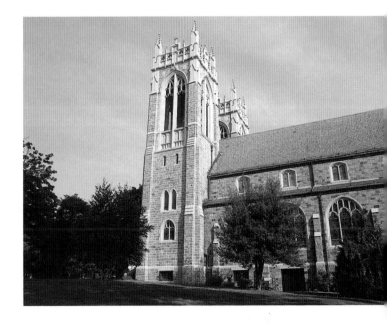

ST. STANISLAUS, BRISTOL

Polish
Established 1919
Current Pastor: Father Brian A. Shaw
Parochial Vicar: Father Lech Kuna
1100 households

At the turn of the century, Polish immigrants were drawn by employment opportunities in the local factories and foundries of Bristol, attending St. Joseph Church. In 1902, their number was sufficient to warrant the formation of the St. Stanislaus Kostka Society. On April 21, 1919, Bishop John J. Nilan named Father George Bartlewski founding pastor of St. Stanislaus Parish. Six days later, Father Bartlewski offered the first parish Mass at town hall. The construction of a basement church climaxed with the blessing of the cornerstone by Bishop Nilan on September 26, 1920. Auxiliary Bishop John G. Murray dedicated the basement church on May 30, 1921. Despite the onset of the national Depression, St. Stanislaus School was constructed and it opened on September 15, 1930, staffed by the Sisters of St. Joseph of the Third Order of St. Francis. In 1954 the basement church was demolished and Masses were temporarily moved to the school hall as plans were made to complete the church. A new Gothic edifice in brick rose on the site of the original church and was dedicated on May 20, 1956. To the dismay of many, rising costs and decreasing enrollment forced the closing of the parish school in 1985.

ST. CATHERINE OF SIENA, BROAD BROOK

Established 1886
Current Pastor: Monsignor David Q. Liptak
Almost 1000 households

In 1827, the Irish laborers working at the nearby Enfield Falls Canal received visits from a New York priest, Father John Power, and in 1828 from a Boston priest, Father Robert D. Woodley. Hartford priests later cared for these immigrants from 1829 to 1852. The first Mass in Broad Brook had been celebrated by Father James Smyth of St. Mary, Windsor Locks. In March 1854, the section became a mission of St. Bernard, Rockville under Father Bernard Tully. Elihu Hubbard offered his house as a site for Mass. He later donated land on Depot Street where St. Patrick mission chapel was built and dedicated by Bishop Francis P. McFarland on April 10, 1864. It still stands today. In 1865, the mission came under Thompsonville's jurisdiction. Circuit Pastor Father John Mulcahy drafted plans for a larger church in Broad Brook. On the land donated in 1880 by Kyran O'Neill, the new church of St. Catherine of Siena was dedicated on June 19, 1881.

St. Joseph, Canaan

Established 1920
Current Pastor: Father James Merlino, O.F.M.
300 households

Attracted by the iron and lime industries, Catholics settled in Canaan during the 1830s. At various times, they were cared for by pastors from New Haven, Bridgeport and Norwalk. It is probable that Father James Smyth from Hartford celebrated Mass at the Canaan home of Patrick Lynch on Christmas Day 1848. Parish history, however, identifies the celebrant as Father John Smith of Albany, New York. By 1851, Canaan's three resident Catholic families were cared for from nearby St. Patrick Church, Falls Village. In 1871, the first St. Joseph Church was built on North Elm Street and dedicated on September 11, 1873. Two years later, Canaan became the mission responsibility of St. Mary, Lakeville. On May 20, 1920, St. Joseph was made a parish by Bishop John J. Nilan, who appointed Father Joseph W. Barry as pastor. Ironically, St. Joseph was now charged with the responsibility for Falls Village, which had reverted to mission status under Lakeville in 1875. Third pastor

Father Daniel J. Manning built a new stone church on Main Street. Bishop Maurice F. McAuliffe dedicated it on October 27, 1940.

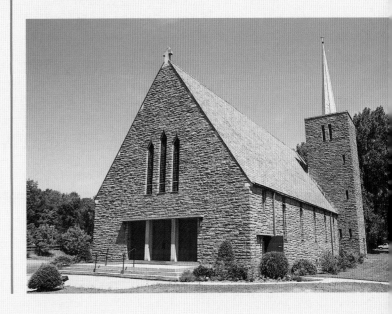

Epiphany, Cheshire

Established 1967
Current Pastor: Father Norman L. Brockett
825 households

Epiphany was established as the first daughter parish of St. Bridget, Cheshire, on September 28, 1967, by Archbishop Henry J. O'Brien. Father Eugene Torpey was appointed founding pastor. The first parish Mass was offered at the Doolittle School on October 1, 1967, with about 300 people participating in the liturgy. In October 1968, Father Torpey broke ground for a parish church on Huckins Road. A year later on October 19, the Church of the Epiphany was dedicated by Archbishop John F. Whealon. A new parish center with a capacity of some 500 was added to the plant and solemnly blessed by Archbishop Whealon on October 17, 1987.

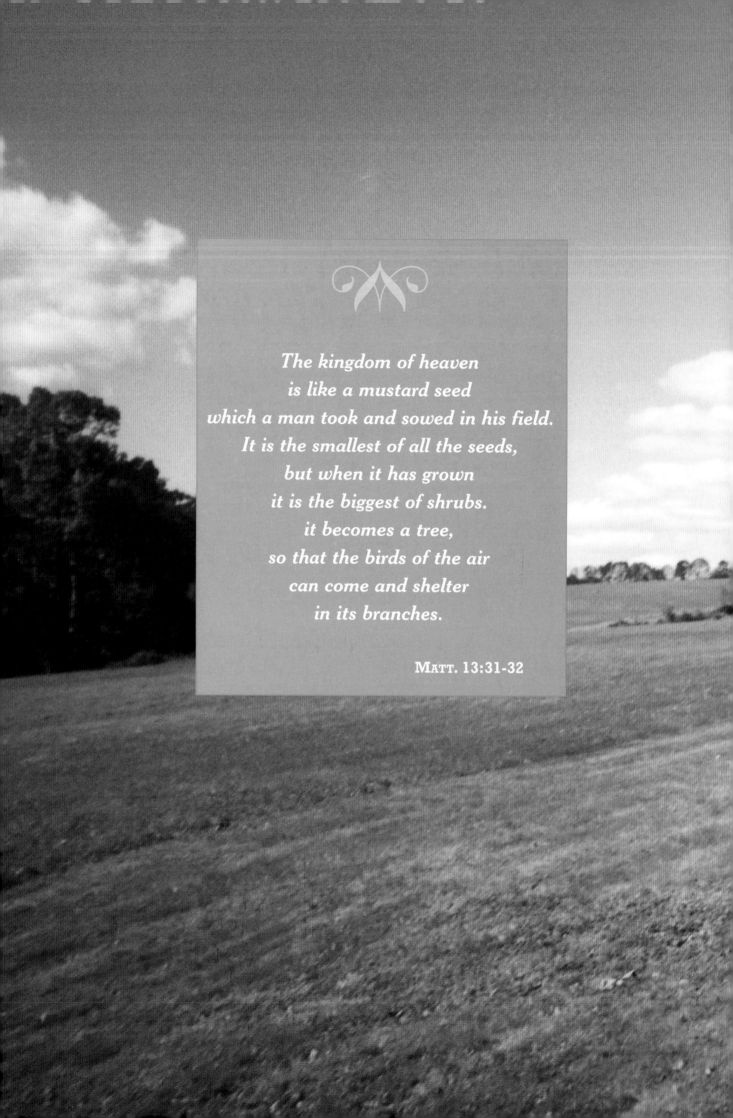

*The kingdom of heaven
is like a mustard seed
which a man took and sowed in his field.
It is the smallest of all the seeds,
but when it has grown
it is the biggest of shrubs.
it becomes a tree,
so that the birds of the air
can come and shelter
in its branches.*

MATT. 13:31-32

ST. BRIDGET, CHESHIRE

Established 1871
Current Pastor: Father James B. Gunnoud
Parochial Vicar: Father Robert P. Ricciardi
2700 households

The first known Mass in Cheshire was offered in 1843 at the Booth Homestead on Meriden Road by Father Bernard Tevin of St. Mary, New Haven. In 1854, Cheshire passed to the care of St. Rose, Meriden, whose pastor, Father Hugh O'Reilly, said Mass on Main Street at Baldwin Hall. In 1855, Father O'Reilly bought an acre of land at Highland Avenue on Route 10. In July 1859, the cornerstone of the St. Bridget mission church was blessed. The first mission Mass was offered by Father Charles McCallion of Meriden on Christmas Day 1859. The church was dedicated on September 29, 1861. From 1859 until 1862, the mission had been entrusted to priests from Wallingford, but it again reverted to Meriden in 1862. Father Thomas Drea was appointed by Bishop Francis P.

McFarland as Cheshire's first resident pastor in 1871. Because of an insufficient Catholic population, Cheshire had once more reverted to mission status and was placed under Southington. The first decades of the 20th century, however, witnessed a Catholic migration to Cheshire that resulted in the appointment of Father Patrick A. McCarthy as pastor of the newly restored St. Bridget Parish in January 1930. On December 7, 1958, the newly built St. Bridget Church was dedicated by Archbishop Henry J. O'Brien. Father Arthur P. Hanley next built a junior high school adjoining the parish hall. It was dedicated on November 24, 1964, and staffed by the Sisters of Charity. When the times later forced the school to close in 1985, the building became a parish center. The school reopened in 1994 and has since grown to twenty-two classrooms, including science and communication centers. A weather station will soon be established.

ST. THOMAS BECKET, CHESHIRE

Established 1971
Current Pastor: Father Eugene J. Charman
About 750 households

St. Thomas Becket began as a mission of St. Bridget, Cheshire, in June 1970 with about 385 families. Father Kenneth J. Frisbie was appointed mission pastor. He offered the first Mass on June 14 at Cheshire High School, where Mass was celebrated until a church was built. Dedication ceremonies for St. Thomas Becket Church occurred on September 30, 1973. The church and parish center complex is located on a five-acre site at North Brooksvale Road. The parish center was dedicated on July 15, 1990, by Archbishop John F. Whealon.

ST. PATRICK, COLLINSVILLE

Established 1856
Current Pastor: Father Ronald P. May
1200 households

The first recorded Mass in Collinsville was offered in 1841 by Hartford pastor Father John Brady. In May 1849, New Britain pastor Father Luke Daly began attending to all Farmington Valley Catholics. The first Catholic church in Collinsville was dedicated by Bishop Bernard O'Reilly on August 22, 1852. Parishioner Peter Meyers donated the land for the church, which was designed by renowned church architect Patrick C. Keely. By December 10, 1856, when Father Patrick J. O'Dwyer was appointed first resident pastor of the newly created St. Patrick parish, the congregation had risen to about 500 from its nucleus of 12 a decade before. In 1925, a fire of unknown origin gutted the church, which was then restored. By 1933, plans were laid for a new stone church. A basement chapel opened in 1934 and the finished superstructure was dedicated by Bishop Maurice F. McAuliffe on November 22, 1936. Father Donald J. O'Leary was a moving force in obtaining the radio tower that made possible the birth of archdiocesan radio station WJMJ in 1976.

ST. BRIDGET, CORNWALL BRIDGE

Established 1883
Current Administrator: Father Francis R. Fador
Almost 200 households

The first Catholic church in West Cornwall was built in 1854 by Father Peter Kelly, pastor at Falls Village. Earlier, Masses had been celebrated at the Cornwall home of Mary O'Rourke Troy. In 1875, Cornwall was transferred to the pastoral care of St. Mary, Lakeville. Under Father Henry Lynch, a new church was dedicated on June 3, 1883, in Cornwall Bridge, four miles south of the original chapel. St. Bridget attained full parish status in 1883, when Father William O'Reilly Sheridan was named first pastor. He completed the church and planned a parish cemetery. After Father James T. Walsh was appointed to Cornwall in 1896, he moved the parochial residence to St. Bernard, Sharon, because of population shifts. Meanwhile, Cornwall reverted to mission status. Ten Sharon pastors subsequently ministered at St. Bridget until January 3, 1935, when Cornwall became the mission of Goshen's newly created St. Thomas parish. On June 29, 1978, St. Bridget was happily raised to parish status with Father L. Randall Blackall named the modern day founding pastor.

ST. PATRICK CHURCH

ST. JUDE, DERBY

Established 1961
Current Pastor: Father William J. Killeen
More than 500 households

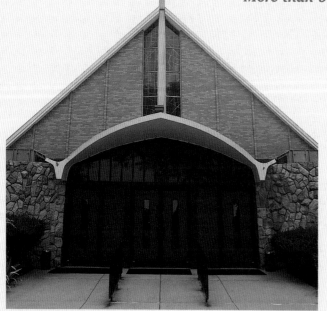

The first recorded Catholic in Derby was Claudius Barthelme, who arrived in 1760. A few years later he was joined by a number of exiled French Acadians. More Catholics settled in the area in 1833. The major influx had arrived by 1880 with Irish immigrants fleeing the potato famines. Catholics of East Derby had been served by circuit priests from New Haven and Waterbury, including the well traveled Father James Smyth. Later, they began to attend St. Mary Church, Derby, which was the mother parish for more than a century. On September 24, 1961, Archbishop Henry J. O'Brien appointed Father Robert G. Keating founding pastor of St. Jude in East Derby. The St. Mary community had given the new parish a 16-acre tract atop Sentinel Hill. A garage on the property was soon renovated for use as a daily chapel. Four days later the first Sunday Mass was celebrated at the Bradley School. Groundbreaking for a new church occurred on May 20 in a ceremony conducted by the pastor and Monsignor John H. Quinn of St. Mary. On May 4, 1963, Archbishop O'Brien dedicated St. Jude Church.

ST. MARY THE IMMACULATE CONCEPTION, DERBY

Established 1851
Current Pastor: Father Edward Pfnausch
1200 households

By 1883 New Haven's Father James McDermott celebrated Mass at the Old Point House on Main Street. On Elizabeth Street land donated by a Mr. Phelps, a church was erected in 1845, though its formal dedication did not occur until May 2, 1852. Immigration soon ensured that local Catholic ranks were sufficient for the appointment of Father James Lynch as first pastor of the newly created parish of St. Mary of the Immaculate Conception on March 31, 1851. Father Lynch expanded parish property and instituted a small, short-lived parochial school in the church basement. Soon, parish growth necessitated a new church. Father Peter M. Kennedy hired the renowned New York architect Patrick C. Keely. The church was dedicated by Bishop Lawrence S. McMahon on November 21, 1883. Father Kennedy later brought the Sisters of Mercy from Meriden to teach in the revived church basement school, which opened September 1, 1885. A new school was finally built and dedicated in September 1898. Under the leadership of Father John Quinn, a new school on Seymour Ave was dedicated in 1954. It later merged with St. Michael School, Derby, in 1988.

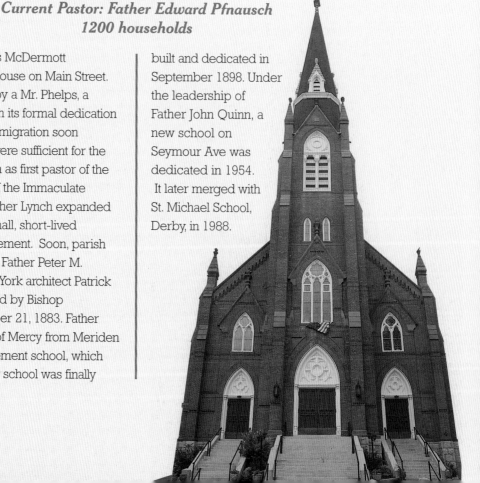

ST. MICHAEL THE ARCHANGEL, DERBY

Polish
Established 1905
Current Pastor: Father Mitchell Wanat, C.M.
Parochial Vicar: Father Joseph Szpilski, C.M.
1100 households

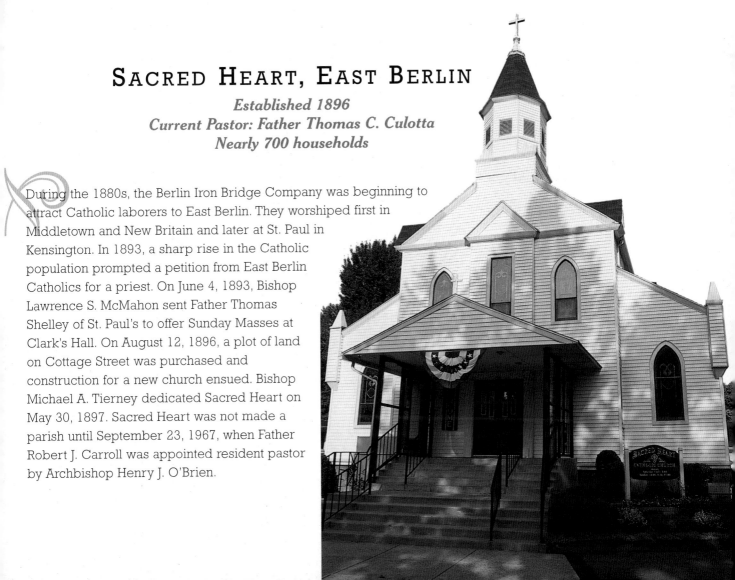

Largely from Austrian Poland, immigrants began arriving in Derby around 1885. Despite a degree of factionalism within the early immigrant community, Francis Stochmal led in founding the Parish Society of St. Michael the Archangel on February 7, 1903. Land on Derby Avenue was bought later that year. Despite the arrival in Derby of Father Walter Stec of Poland, both Bishop Michael A. Tierney and the Apostolic Delegate, to whom the Poles appealed still refused permission for a new parish. Father Stec soon returned to Poland. Nevertheless, fear of schism and the belated support of St. Mary pastor Father Charles J. McElroy persuaded Bishop Tierney to establish St. Michael the Archangel parish on July 15, 1905. Father Stanislaus Konieczny, C.M., of the Vincentian Fathers was appointed founding pastor. Durrschmidt Hall on lower Main Street was rented for Masses, the first of which was celebrated on August 20, 1905. A new church was dedicated on July 4, 1907, by Father John Synnott, who represented Bishop Tierney. Succeeding the founding pastor in 1906, Father Paul W. Waszko, C.M., built a school staffed by the Sisters of the Holy Family of Nazareth and dedicated on January 1, 1915. The school merged with St. Mary School, Derby in 1988.

SACRED HEART, EAST BERLIN

Established 1896
Current Pastor: Father Thomas C. Culotta
Nearly 700 households

During the 1880s, the Berlin Iron Bridge Company was beginning to attract Catholic laborers to East Berlin. They worshiped first in Middletown and New Britain and later at St. Paul in Kensington. In 1893, a sharp rise in the Catholic population prompted a petition from East Berlin Catholics for a priest. On June 4, 1893, Bishop Lawrence S. McMahon sent Father Thomas Shelley of St. Paul's to offer Sunday Masses at Clark's Hall. On August 12, 1896, a plot of land on Cottage Street was purchased and construction for a new church ensued. Bishop Michael A. Tierney dedicated Sacred Heart on May 30, 1897. Sacred Heart was not made a parish until September 23, 1967, when Father Robert J. Carroll was appointed resident pastor by Archbishop Henry J. O'Brien.

St. Michael the Archangel,
Derby, Window

ENT CHURCH

BLESSED SACRAMENT, EAST HARTFORD

Established 1948
Current Pastor: Father Jeffrey T. Walsh
430 households

The first pastor of the newly created Blessed Sacrament Church was Father Henry J. Murphy. At first, it was not necessary to build a church, because in 1947 the chancery had erected a rectangular structure made of cinder block with a seating capacity of about 250. But soon the rapid increase of parishioners created problems. In the post World War II years, a housing boom within Blessed Sacrament's territory and wide employment opportunities at nearby Pratt and Whitney Aircraft attracted a large number of French-Canadians to the area. In 1955, relentless growth necessitated the establishment of a mission church, St. Christopher's, which Father Murphy tended to in addition to the mother parish. On May 7, 1972, Archbishop John F. Whealon dedicated the modern Blessed Sacrament Church. In 1988, a large parish center was built, containing classrooms, offices, and a gymnasium-hall.

OUR LADY OF PEACE, EAST HARTFORD

Established 1971
Current Pastor: Father James J. Nock
Almost 700 households

In June 1970, Archbishop John F. Whealon surprised the parishioners of St. Christopher parish, East Hartford, with an announcement. From the territory of this large parish, a mission would be established in the southern segment adjoining the town of Glastonbury. About 650 families would be included in the mission area. Father Leo Maynard was named mission pastor. On June 13, 1970, Father Maynard offered the mission's first Mass at the Dr. Thomas O'Connell School on May Road. Mass would be offered there until a church was built. The blessing of full canonical status came on April 23, 1971, as the mission of St. Christopher became the parish of Our Lady of Peace. In September of the following year, 11 acres of land were purchased on May Road as the site for the church. Groundbreaking on the May Road acreage occurred on May 26, 1974. Finally, the first Mass was offered in the new church on May 24, 1975. On June 22 of that year, Archbishop Whealon dedicated Our Lady of Peace Church.

St. Isaac Jogues, East Hartford

Established 1964
Current Pastor: Father Emilio P. Padelli
1050 households

St. Christopher, East Hartford

Established 1965
Current Pastor: Father James G. Fanelli
1200 households

World War II brought people to East Hartford from all over New England to seek employment at Pratt and Whitney Aircraft. With the eastern portion of St. Rose parish swelling, its pastor, Father Austin Munich, began to say Mass for this new segment of the population at the community building on Cannon Road. The first Mass was celebrated on December 25, 1944. Finally, a mission church of St. Isaac Jogues, located on Laurel Park Heights, was dedicated on May 2, 1964, by Archbishop Henry J. O'Brien. The new edifice became the first in New England to be constructed of pre-cast tilt up concrete panels. Its design reflects the simple, rustic life and environment of the American frontier where St. Isaac Jogues carried on his missionary work in New York State. St. Isaac Jogues attained full canonical status in 1965.

An increase in population within Blessed Sacrament parish, East Hartford, occasioned the creation of a mission in 1955 at the direction of Archbishop Henry J. O'Brien. Father Henry J. Murphy, pastor of Blessed Sacrament, was made responsible for the mission. By December 1955, the cornerstone of St. Christopher mission church had been formally blessed. Until St. Christopher attained full parish status on September 16, 1965, the indefatigable Father Murphy served both Blessed Sacrament and its mission. He had opened

St. Christopher School on Brewer Street in 1963, staffed by the Sisters of Jesus Christ Crucified from Brockton, Massachusetts. When St. Christopher became a parish, Father Murphy became the first resident pastor, renting a private home until construction of a rectory near the church could be completed. With the departure of the sisters in 1989, lay teachers staffed St. Christopher's School, with a Dominican Sister as principal.

St. Mary, East Hartford

Established 1873
Current Pastor: Father Martin J. Scholsky
Parochial Vicar: Father Frank Papa, S.O.L.T.
1100 households

The largely Irish constituency of East Hartford was served by Hartford's St. Patrick Church. From 1860 to 1870, Catholic growth east of the Connecticut River was so pronounced that the liturgy was celebrated for the first time at Main Street's Elm Hall on July 6, 1873, by Father James Hughes of St. Patrick. On August 1 of that year Father Patrick F. Goodwin was appointed by Bishop Francis P. McFarland as first pastor of the new St. Mary parish. His spacious jurisdiction included South Windsor, Wethersfield, Glastonbury, and Rocky Hill. Father John A. Mulcahy began church construction on a parcel of land at the northeast corner of Main Street and Woodbridge Avenue. St. Mary Church was dedicated by Bishop Thomas Galberry on November 11, 1877. Not intimidated by the national Depression, the parish built a school under Father Thomas Drennan. Cornerstone ceremonies were held in September 1929. The new school opened on September 8, 1930, staffed by the Sisters of Mercy. The school would close in 1973. Father John W. Dial built the modern St. Mary Church, dedicated by Archbishop Henry J. O'Brien on December 22, 1962.

St. Rose of Lima, East Hartford

Established 1920
Current Pastor: Father Thomas R. Mitchell
776 households

On October 25, 1920, St. Rose was made a parish in the Burnside section of East Hartford. Its territory was taken from St. Mary parish. Father Alexander Mitchell was appointed first pastor by Bishop John J. Nilan. He secured 10 acres of land that stretched from the western corner of Burnside Avenue down Church Street. With the labor of his parishioners, Father Mitchell was soon able to build a frame church in the form of a Quonset hut situated between the present church and Burnside Avenue. Father Mitchell then built a more spacious structure on Church Street, dedicated on June 22, 1924. As the number of parish youngsters grew, the pastor began work on a long anticipated parochial school. In 1954, he purchased two pieces of property, which included a building, across from St. Rose's at 20 Church Street. The dwelling was refurbished as a convent for the Sisters of Notre Dame de Namur, who would staff the new school. Construction then moved forward. St. Rose Junior High School opened on November 28, 1955 and was dedicated by Archbishop Henry J. O'Brien on December 11.

Our Lady of Pompeii, East Haven

Established 1947
Current Pastor: Father David J. Borino
2300 households

Around 1912, Father Robert L. Rumaggi, O.P., from St. Mary, New Haven, began offering Mass in private homes in East Haven's Foxon area. He raised funds for a permanent chapel. Soon the Russo family donated land, cash and a church bell for the chapel. By 1922, the Foxon section had a place of worship at the corner of Old Foxon Road and Brennan Street. The chapel was placed under the patronage of Our Lady of the Rosary of Pompeii. At this time Foxon was a mission of St. Barnabas, North Haven. By 1938, Foxon formally became a mission of St. Therese Church, North Haven. On December 13, 1947, Our Lady of Pompeii Chapel was incorporated but still remained a mission. On February 7, 1957, Archbishop Henry J. O'Brien raised Our Lady of Pompeii to a full parish and appointed Father John P. O'Neill as first resident pastor. Anticipating events while still pastor at St. Therese, Father O'Neill had purchased seven acres of land for a new church on Route 80 from William Zuckerman in November 1956. The new Our Lady of Pompeii Church was dedicated by Archbishop O'Brien

on March 25, 1961. The old chapel was completely destroyed by fire in 1963, the cause unknown.

St. Clare, East Haven

Established 1947
Current Pastor: Father Ralph M. Colicchio
More than 700 households

Catholics of East Haven's Momauguin section first attended Mass at a hall over a blacksmith's shop. The hall was rented following the establishment of St. Vincent de Paul Parish in October 1914. By 1916, however, they were attending the newly built St. Vincent de Paul Church. But soon priests from the mother parish were celebrating summer Masses at the George Street firehouse or Swift's Hotel in Momauguin. On May 31, 1947, St. Clare Parish was formally created by then Bishop Henry J.

O'Brien, who appointed Father John F. O'Donnell first pastor. The new pastor moved swiftly, buying land on Coe Avenue. The newly constructed St. Clare Church was dedicated on February 27, 1949. The times eventually called for new church construction. On August 27, 1966, Archbishop O'Brien dedicated the new St. Clare Church, located on Coe Avenue. The old church was converted into a hall.

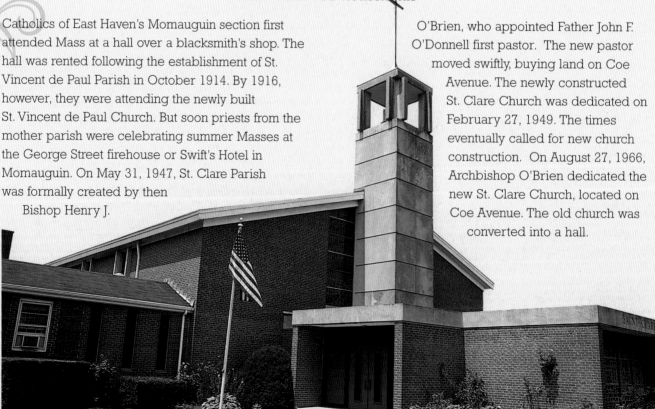

ST. VINCENT DE PAUL, EAST HAVEN

Established 1915
Current Pastor: Father Gary F. Simeone
Pastor Emeritus: Father Robert J. Burbank. Parochial Vicar: Father Dariusz Gosciniak
More than 2600 households

For East Haven Catholics, the founding of St. Vincent de Paul parish on October 9, 1914, by Bishop John J. Nilan alleviated the burden of travel to New Haven's St. Francis Church. Appointed first pastor, Father Michael L. Reagan celebrated the initial Masses in a hall over a blacksmith's shop until the parish church was erected at Main Street and Charter Oak Avenue. It was dedicated by Bishop Nilan on June 27, 1915. In 1938, Father Jeremiah J. Broderick built a new church alongside the parochial residence, dedicated by Bishop Maurice F. McAuliffe. In 1958 Father Leo W. Weston purchased properties adjoining the church site for a school and a new convent. Groundbreaking ceremonies were held on March 25, 1962, and the school was dedicated by Archbishop Henry J. O'Brien on August 4, 1963.

ST. PHILIP, EAST WINDSOR

Established 1959
Current Administrator: Father Adam Subocz
330 households

A few years before St. Philip parish was born, a committee of St. Mary Church, Windsor Locks, had proposed a mission at Warehouse Point. On August 3, 1959, a parcel of land on Bridge Street was purchased. On November 19, Archbishop Henry J. O'Brien appointed Father Thomas H. Dwyer as founding pastor of St. Philip the Apostle Parish. The East Windsor Board of Education granted the use of the high school auditorium for Sunday Mass. The pastor celebrated the first parish Mass on November 19, 1959, for a congregation of 525. Archbishop O'Brien dedicated a new chapel in the rectory on October 5, 1960. Ground was broken for St. Philip church on July 22 at the old Daly farm on Route 5. On August 17, 1963, St. Philip's was solemnly dedicated by Archbishop O'Brien.

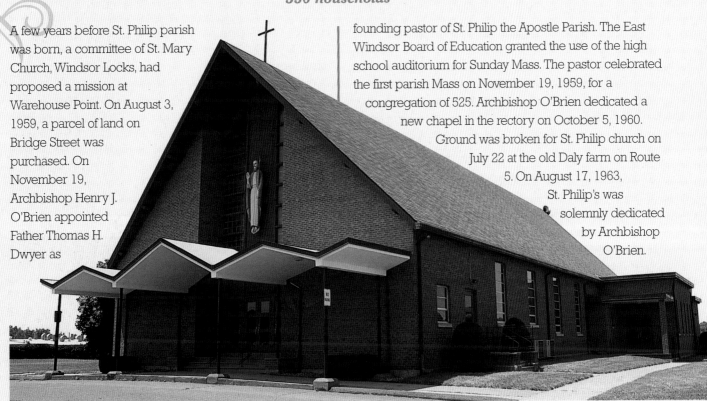

HOLY FAMILY, ENFIELD

Established 1965
Current Pastor: Father Francis T. Kerwan
2600 households

Holy Family, Enfield, was the last church dedicated during the episcopate of Archbishop Henry J. O'Brien. He established the parish on September 16, 1965, appointing Father Francis T. Kerwan founding pastor. About 20 acres on Simon Road had already been purchased as the site of a church. More than 1200 households comprised the new parish. Father Kerwan celebrated the first parish Mass at Enfield High School on September 19, 1965. In the spring of 1966, a church building fund campaign was launched. On July 9, 1967, ground was broken and construction began. On November 9, 1968, the church of trapezoidal design was dedicated by Auxiliary Bishop John F. Hackett.

ST. ADALBERT, ENFIELD

Polish
Established 1915
Current Pastor: Father Edmund M. O'Brien
600 households

Employed primarily at the major local industry, Bigelow-Sanford carpet mill, Polish immigrants first worshiped at St. Michael Chapel in the basement of St. Patrick Church. On September 1, 1907, Bishop Michael A. Tierney made Father Paul W. Piechocki responsible for the immigrants. Father Piechocki soon persuaded Bishop John J. Nilan to buy land on Alden Avenue as the prospective site of a Polish church. Bishop Nilan established St. Adalbert parish on January 17, 1915. Father Stanislaus Federkiewicz was named first pastor. St. Michael's Chapel remained in use until the new Polish church was constructed on Alden Avenue. Father Federkiewicz blessed the cornerstone of St. Adalbert on October 10, 1915. The first Mass was offered in the unfinished church basement on Christmas 1915. Bishop Nilan dedicated the lower church on May 7, 1916. Finally, the completed St. Adalbert was dedicated by Bishop Maurice F. McAuliffe on July 8, 1928. Felician sisters staffed the parish school, which began with a kindergarten conducted in the church basement. On May 11, 1958, ground was broken for a separate school building. The completed school was dedicated by Auxiliary Bishop John F. Hackett on August 16, 1959.

Synnott became the first resident pastor of St. Bernard as it was raised to parish status by Bishop McMahon. Father Edward J. Reardon erected a new church on the site of the demolished old one, which was too small to accommodate the congregation. Archbishop Henry J. O'Brien officiated at the dedication in 1956. Father Reardon also erected a parish school in 1958 on Hazard Avenue, staffed by the Felician Sisters.

ST. BERNARD, ENFIELD

Established 1870
Current Pastor: Father Joseph E. Vujs
Parochial Vicar: Father William F. O'Keefe
1300 households

Until 1852 when Hazardville passed to the care of Windsor Locks, the section was tended by Hartford priests. About 1860, the Maple Street home of William Casey became the site of Hazardville's first Mass. The celebrant was Father James Smyth of St. Mary, Windsor Locks. In January 1863, Hazardville became the pastoral responsibility of St. Patrick parish, Thompsonville. In 1865, with an old schoolhouse outfitted for Mass, formal worship came closer to reality in Hazardville. Father John A. Mulcahy proceeded to build a church on Main Street. Bishop Lawrence S. McMahon blessed the cornerstone on September 12, 1880, and the church was dedicated on July 17, 1891. In 1888, Father John

ST. MARTHA, ENFIELD

Established 1961
Current Pastor: Father John P. Gwozdz
1400 households

St. Martha, Enfield, was established by Archbishop Henry J. O'Brien in September 1961. Appointed founding pastor, Father John B. O'Connell offered the first parish Mass at the Knights of Columbus Hall on September 24. St. Martha was a parish with an initially large congregation and a 20-acre tract on Brainard Road, purchased earlier by the chancery. The pastor later secured 20 additional acres contiguous with the first parcel. When an early parish census revealed the presence of many young families, the congregation opted to build a school and use its auditorium as a temporary church. On December 15, 1962, Father Thomas Dwyer of nearby St. Philip Church, Warehouse Point, delivered an address on the occasion of the groundbreaking for the new St. Martha complex. The first parish Mass in the auditorium-style church was held on August 4, 1963. Archbishop O'Brien dedicated St. Martha Church and School on September 22 of that year.

ST. PATRICK, ENFIELD

Established 1866
Current Pastor: Father Richard Welch, C. Ss.R.
Parochial Vicar: Father Thomas G. Sullivan, C. Ss.R.
1200 households

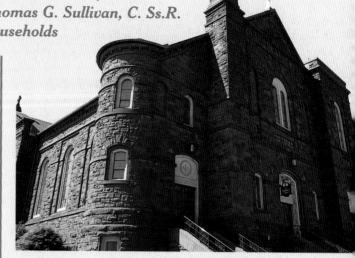

In the fall of 1831, Father James Fitton of Hartford offered a dawn Mass at the home of Richard Murphy in the Thompsonville section of Enfield. Because of prejudice, there was no regular Mass scheduled in Thompsonville until 1834. By 1850, Father James Smyth of Windsor Locks tended Thompsonville from St. Mary Church. The town hall was now the site of monthly Mass. He built a mission church at Pearl and Cross Streets in 1860 as the Catholic population rose. Father John Cooney organized a two-room school, named for St. Joseph, in the church basement. Lay teachers conducted classes for about one year and were succeeded by Sisters of Mercy from Hartford. Parish needs required a larger school, which opened in September 1874. Father John A. Mulcahy purchased property at Pearl and High Streets for a new church. Father Patrick Donahoe secured a public school edifice to serve for parochial education and moved the structure to property adjacent to the parish convent. Father Joseph Gleason completed the new church basement, whose cornerstone was blessed on August 16 1892. The finished church was dedicated by Bishop Michael A. Tierney on November 20, 1904. Tragedy struck on January 5, 1949, when a fire ignited by a vigil light completely gutted St. Patrick, leaving only the external walls standing. Historic St. Patrick was fully restored by November 12, 1950. Father Kilcoyne built a new 16-room school, still known as St. Joseph in 1958. It closed in 1996.

ST. PATRICK MISSION, FALLS VILLAGE

Established 1851
Current Mission Priest: Father James Merlino, O.F.M.
40 households

In 1849, the first Mass in this rustic village within Canaan was celebrated by Father John C. Brady, pastor of St. Mary, Norwalk. Father Christopher Moore was then named first resident pastor of St. Patrick parish, Falls Village. Father Peter Kelly built the first St. Patrick Church in 1854. Father Henry J. Lynch moved the parish seat to nearby Salisbury and St. Patrick reverted to the status of a mission of Lakeville's new St. Mary Parish. After the old St. Patrick's Church was destroyed by fire in 1914, a new church was built and dedicated in November 1915 by Bishop John J. Nilan. In 1920, St. Patrick Mission was made a mission of the newly created St. Joseph, Canaan, a relationship that remains today.

ST. PATRICK, FARMINGTON

Established 1871
Current Pastor: Father James F. Pilon
1600 households

In the 19th century, Farmington Catholics were cared for by Father John Brady of Hartford and after 1848 by Father Luke Daly of New Britain. When St. Joseph, Bristol, became a parish in 1864, Farmington was administered by its pastor, Father Michael Rodden. Within four years, he was succeeded by Father Patrick Duggett, who in 1870 bought an old building on Farmington Avenue to serve as the town's first Catholic Church. In 1885, Farmington became Plainville's mission under the care of Father Henry Walsh. In the fall of 1918, Bishop John J. Nilan made St. Patrick's a parish with Father M. Ernest Wilson as first pastor. Bishop Nilan instructed Father Wilson to build a new church on a Main Street site chosen by the prelate himself. With much help from his parishioners, the pastor soon had a basement church constructed and dedicated on November 27, 1919. The completed superstructure was dedicated on June 11, 1922.

ST. MATTHEW, FORESTVILLE

Established 1891
Current Pastor: Father Brian W. Monnerat
Parochial Vicar: Father Kevin M. Dillon
In residence: Father Francis W. Wright, C.S.Sp.
3000 households

In 1837, a copper mine in Burlington acted as a magnet for Irish immigrants seeking work. In 1848, these immigrants asked Father Luke Daly of New Britain to offer Sunday Mass. He celebrated the first Mass at the Igoe home. When the Burlington mine shut down during the depression of 1857, the immigrants relocated to Forestville and Bristol for jobs on the incoming railroad or in the clock factory. Forestville became the responsibility of St. Joseph, Bristol, in 1864, and later of Our Lady of Mercy, Plainville, in 1891. On November 5, 1891, ground was broken on a Church Avenue plot donated by James Hart Welch. Bishop Lawrence S. McMahon blessed the cornerstone on January 17, 1892. Bishop Michael A. Tierney dedicated the completed structure on June 27, 1897. On October 19, 1918, Forestville was made a parish, with Father William P. Laflin appointed first resident pastor. Father Raymond Mulcahy bought Church Avenue property for a school and convent. On October 1, 1961, Auxiliary Bishop John F. Hackett dedicated St. Matthew School, staffed by the Servants of the Immaculate Heart of Mary. A new St. Matthew's church was built at the corner of Brown Street and Church Avenue, dedicated on May 24, 1987.

St. Dunstan, Glastonbury

Established 1971
Current Pastor: Father William L. Traxl
Parochial Vicar: Father Arthur J. Audet
1350 households

The expansion of population in East Glastonbury resulted in Archbishop John F. Whealon's decision in 1970 to create a new parish there, with Father Joseph R. Bannon appointed first pastor. At first, the infant congregation would be a mission of St. Paul Church, with St. Dunstan as its patron. Sunday Mass was offered at Gideon Welles School until the church was built. On March 21, 1971, St. Dunstan was accorded full parish status. Parish development accelerated with the announcement that land for a church had been purchased in February 1972. On September 30, 1973, hundreds of parishioners applauded Father Bannon's breaking ground for St. Dunstan's on seven acres on Manchester Road. On November 24, 1974, Archbishop Whealon dedicated the new church.

St. Paul, Glastonbury

Established 1954
Current Pastor: Father Kevin P. Cavanaugh
Parochial Vicar: Father John P. Melnick
2000 households

Glastonbury's earliest Catholics traveled to St. Peter Church in Hartford during the 1860's. For a few years, Manchester priests assumed pastoral responsibility for Glastonbury. Portland clerics had a year's jurisdiction until St. Mary, East Hartford, was organized in 1873. Glastonbury became its responsibility until 1902, when it was made a mission of St. Augustine, South Glastonbury. Father Francis Murray of St. Augustine purchased land on Naubuc Avenue where St. Paul Church was built. Bishop Michael A. Tierney blessed the cornerstone on May 31, 1903. Formal ceremonies of dedication occurred on October 18. On September 23, 1954, Archbishop Henry J. O'Brien made St. Paul a parish, with Father Robert P. Sullivan as resident pastor. Ground was broken on November 28, 1956, for a new church. Cornerstone and dedication solemnities were conducted by Archbishop O'Brien on January 25, 1958, for the new church.

St. Thomas of Villanova, Goshen

Established 1880
Current Pastor: Father Raymond G. Proulx
400 households

By the early 19th century, Catholics had settled in Goshen. In 1832, Goshen passed to the care of New Haven. By 1842, Goshen became the responsibility of Bridgeport, then of Norwalk (1848) and finally of Falls Village (1851). Goshen's first recorded Mass was celebrated by Father Peter Kelly of Falls Village in 1854 at the William Devlin home. In August 1856, the priest

received a quarter acre of land from Simon Scoville. Father Kelly then erected a chapel on the land and named the mission St. Columcille. Falls Village pastors celebrated Mass periodically in Goshen until December 1, 1873, when St. Columcille passed to St. Joseph, Winsted. Father Leo Rizzo da Saracena, O.F.M., built a new church that opened on December 8, 1877. The mission was named for St. Thomas of Villanova at the request of Bishop Thomas F. Galberry. In 1882, St. Thomas became a mission of St. Anthony, Litchfield. By 1920, the mission was closed after the Catholic population dwindled. Soon after summer tourism brought seasonal use of the mission in June 1930, St. Thomas reopened. St. Thomas finally gained parish status on December 1, 1934, with Father James Egan appointed pastor. Father Walter Pransketis was able to build a new church dedicated on October 6, 1973, by Archbishop John F. Whealon.

St. Therese, Granby

Established 1958
Current Pastor: Father Ronald R. Yelle
750 households

Irish immigrants first settled on North Granby farms in the 1840s. Later, in the 1880s, Lithuanian and Polish immigrants arrived. St. Bernard church in Tariffville was the nearest Catholic church, but the journey was difficult. On January 10, 1945, eight people met at St. Bernard's rectory with pastor Father John T. O'Connor to plan a Granby mission for about 75 Catholic families. On August 20, 1950, a small white frame chapel at the intersection of West and North Granby Roads was dedicated to St. Therese. In 1958, Archbishop Henry J. O'Brien appointed Father Leonard F. White as first resident pastor, raising St. Therese to full parish status. On June 24, 1973, Archbishop John F. Whealon dedicated a new church on a 22-acre tract located on West Granby Road. In 1985, a new parish center was built.

St. George, Guilford

Established 1870
Current Pastor: Father Lawrence S. Symolon
Parochial Vicar: Father Christopher M. Ford
3300 households

In 1852, Father James P. Cahill of Rhode Island attended Irish immigrants along the New Haven railroad line. Two years later, a priest from St. Patrick, New Haven, offered the first Guilford Mass in a historic stone dwelling dating from 1639. By 1859, the town had become a mission of Branford. Town Catholics bought a store on Whitfield Street for use as a chapel. The first Mass was offered there on March 4, 1860. The new Catholic chapel was deeded by George Hill to Bishop Francis P. McFarland in 1861. On November 11, 1876, the cornerstone of a new church at the corner of Whitfield and High Streets was blessed in the presence of 2000 people. Mass was first offered in the new St. George in 1878 for its congregation of 30 families. St. George was made a parish on March 1, 1887, with Father John H. Dolan appointed resident pastor. In 1956, the Page-Bonzano property on the town green was purchased. Archbishop Henry J. O'Brien dedicated the new church on July 8, 1962. A parish center which has become the focal point for the numerous parish activities that exist here was dedicated in 1983 by Auxiliary Bishop John F. Hackett.

Ascension, Hamden

Established 1964
Current Pastor: Father Thomas J. O'Rourke
Nearly 500 households

Ascension parish, Hamden, was established in 1964 by Archbishop Henry J. O'Brien, with Father John F. Cotter appointed founding pastor. Father Cotter offered the first parish Masses at the Dunbar Hill School. The land for Ascension's parish plant was purchased by the chancery in 1954. Consisting of 27 acres, the tract was the former Benham farm on Dunbar Hill Road. On September 8, 1968, Ascension Church and the Father Cotter Parish Center were dedicated by Auxiliary Bishop Joseph F. Donnelly.

BLESSED SACRAMENT, HAMDEN

Established 1939
Current Pastor: Father Donald J. French
2000 households

Blessed Sacrament parish, Hamden, was created by Bishop Maurice F. McAuliffe on June 8, 1938. Father Charles M. Kavanagh was appointed founding pastor. On April 2, 1939, ground was broken for a church, and construction began. Meanwhile, Blessed Sacrament's first Masses were celebrated in the auditorium of Church Street School. On October 8, 1939, Bishop McAuliffe blessed the cornerstone of Blessed Sacrament Church at Circular Avenue and Church Street. The first Mass in the new church was offered on Christmas Day 1939. Blessed Sacrament was formally dedicated on April 7, 1940. In 1956, Father Daniel J. Barry bought property across Circular Avenue as the future site of a parish school. The former convent became headquarters for the archdiocesan Cana and Family Life Movement. In April 1964, a new chapter of parish history commenced with groundbreaking for a junior high school. The Missionary Zealatrices of the Sacred Heart would staff this parochial institution. Archbishop Henry J. O'Brien dedicated Blessed

Sacrament Junior High School on October 17, 1965. In 1992, the renamed Rev. Daniel J. Barry Junior High School closed its doors.

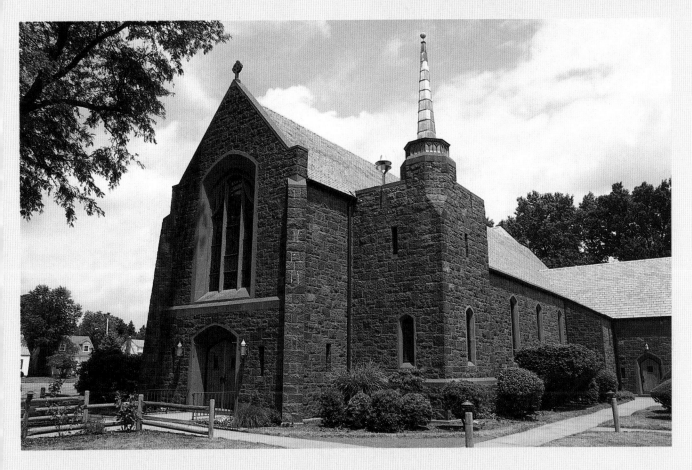

Our Lady of Mt. Carmel, Hamden

Established 1869
Current Pastor: Father Daniel J. Sullivan
Parochial Vicar: Father Daniel G. Keefe
2200 households

The earliest settlers of Hamden named their section Mount Carmel out of reverence for the Bible. Father Matthew Hart commuted from St. Mary, New Haven, to offer the first Mass in Hamden at the home of Parson Iyes around September 1852. On March 1, 1856, the pastor of St. Mary's bought the old Axel Company building and a quarter acre of land on Whitney Avenue. In rotating sequence, New Haven, Wallingford, Southington, and Meriden pastors served the Mount Carmel area in the ensuing years. Wallingford pastor Father Hugh Mallon purchased a Whitney Avenue site for a larger church on January 8, 1872. Bishop Lawrence S. McMahon cemented the cornerstone of a new church on October 17, 1889. Originally, the Hamden mission had been known as St. Mary. On April 26, 1891, Our Lady of Mt. Carmel became a parish, with Father John T. Winters appointed pastor by Bishop McMahon. In January 1957 Father Thomas O'Connell announced plans for the construction of a new church to accommodate the growing congregation. On December 5, 1959, modern day Our Lady of Mt. Carmel Church was dedicated by Archbishop Henry J. O'Brien.

St. Ann, Hamden

Italian
Established 1919
Current Pastor: Father Kenneth P. Bonadies
200 households

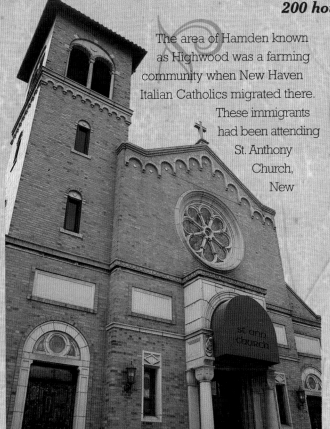

The area of Hamden known as Highwood was a farming community when New Haven Italian Catholics migrated there. These immigrants had been attending St. Anthony Church, New Haven, an Italian parish administered by the Scalabrinian missionaries. Bishop John J. Nilan asked these priests to establish a mission in Highwood. Under Father Bartolomeo Maranchino's direction, an old firehouse on Morse Street was bought and refurbished as a chapel. There, around November 1910, Father Maranchino celebrated the first mission Mass. In October 1920, the Highwood mission of St. Ann was made a parish, with Father Angelo A. Perrone named pastor. In 1925 Father Alvaro Santolini purchased farmland for a church at the corner of Dixwell Avenue and Arch Street. The new edifice was dedicated by Bishop Nilan in May 1927. In 1967, Father William R. Facciuto bought land on Jones Road and built a parish center. Today, St. Ann's is a center for Korean Catholics, the first parish in the Archdiocese selected by Connecticut Koreans as their official religious headquarters.

St. Joan of Arc, Hamden

Established 1971
Current Pastor: Father Robert G. Heffernan
600 households

St. Joan of Arc, Hamden, began in early June 1970 as a mission of Our Lady of Mount Carmel Parish. Its territory was cut from the northern section of Hamden and passed to the care of Father Edgar J. Farrell. The first pastor was responsible for about 500 families. The first community liturgies were celebrated at the Alice Peck School gymnasium on Hillfield Road. The mission community soon voted to adopt St. Joan of Arc as its patron. The mission owned 11.8 acres of land for a future church and rectory on West Todd Street. The mission was accorded parish status by Archbishop John F. Whealon on May 11, 1971. St. Joan of Arc Church was completed on October 18, 1974, and dedicated that December. The parish built a new center and named it in honor of the founding pastor in December of 1990.

St. Rita, Hamden

Established 1928
Current Pastor: Monsignor David M. Walker
Parochial Vicar: Father Vincent J. Curran
2000 households

St. Rita Parish, Hamden, began as a mission of Our Lady of Mount Carmel. On December 9, 1923, Mount Carmel pastor Father Francis E. May opened a mission chapel on Park Avenue. Bishop John J. Nilan conducted the dedication ceremonies that day. A one-story church on Whitney Avenue replaced the chapel and was dedicated on December 8, 1929. On February 3, 1932, Father Matthew F. Brady became first pastor as St. Rita became a parish. The name had been chosen earlier by Father May, who had completed his studies for the priesthood as St. Rita was canonized.

On May 2, 1945, five Sisters of Notre Dame de Namur arrived to supervise religious instruction for parish youngsters. A residence had been purchased at Whitney Avenue and Waite Street for the sisters. In 1954, Father Downey bought land on Whitney Avenue for a parochial school. On June 17, 1956, Archbishop Henry J. O'Brien dedicated St. Rita School. By the 1960s an extensive parish revenue drive was organized to build a new church. The decision was made to build modern St. Rita above the lower church. The new building was dedicated on December 6, 1964, by Archbishop Henry J. O'Brien.

St. Stephen, Hamden

Established 1953
Current Pastor: Father David J. Baranowski
400 households

On June 18, 1915, Bishop John J. Nilan appointed Father Charles F. Kelly of St. Francis, New Haven, to minister to the State Street section of Hamden as a mission. Ground was broken on State Street for the church of St. Stephen on July 19, 1915. On August 22nd, Father Kelly celebrated the first Mass in the little wooden edifice. In December 1915, St. Stephen became a mission of St. Donato, New Haven, where Father Kelly was then pastor. The chapel was belatedly dedicated on May 3, 1917.

In 1920, St. Stephen's passed to the care of St. Barnabas, North Haven, whose pastor was Father Thomas Sullivan. In 1953, Archbishop Henry J. O'Brien made St. Stephen an independent parish, with Father Albert Taylor as resident pastor. In 1956, Father Taylor broke ground for the modern St. Stephen church on Ridge Road, which was later dedicated by Archbishop O'Brien on September 28, 1957. In September 1964, the newly constructed St. Stephen School opened, staffed by the Sisters of Mercy.

CATHEDRAL OF ST. JOSEPH, HARTFORD

Established 1872
Current Pastor: Monsignor Daniel J. Plocharczyk
500 households

Old Cathedral

At the time of its creation, the Diocese of Hartford included Connecticut and Rhode Island. With the separation of the two states in 1872, Bishop Francis P. McFarland made Hartford his seat. His residence was a stately home at the corner of Woodland and Collins Streets, occupied on March 6, 1872. On July 17 of that year, he bought the Morgan-Goodwin property on Farmington Avenue, intending eventually to erect a cathedral, a residence, and a motherhouse for the Sisters of Mercy. The convent was built first, and on November 26, 1873, Bishop McFarland dedicated the convent chapel to St. Joseph, which served as the pro-cathedral. Bishop Thomas Galberry, O.S.A., broke ground for the cathedral on Farmington Avenue on August 30, 1876. He blessed the cornerstone on

April 29, 1877. At his accession in 1876, he had chosen to use St. Peter church as a pro-cathedral until the cathedral basement was ready, which would be on February 10, 1878. On May 8, 1892, St. Joseph Cathedral was formally consecrated by Bishop Lawrence S. McMahon. The architect of the Gothic brownstone design was the famed Patrick C. Keely of New York. The Cathedral became the centerpiece of the parish plant that included a convent, a rectory built in 1875 and the parish school built in 1878. St. Joseph School was located at the corner of Capitol Avenue and Broad Street, opening on January 13, 1879. A major addition to the parish was the new school on Asylum Avenue, blessed on September 7, 1924. The Broad Street building was sold to Holy Trinity parish in 1924. The Sisters of Mercy staffed the entire school, since the Christian Brothers, who had been in charge of a tentative high school, had departed in 1910. On December 31, 1956, a fire of suspicious origin completely destroyed the historic brownstone building. With a motto of "Fire Destroys, Faith Rebuilds", a mighty fundraising campaign began. While construction proceeded, cathedral parishioners attended Mass first at the state armory and then at the auditorium of the nearby Aetna Life Insurance Company. During this time, St. Lawrence O'Toole Church served as pro-cathedral. On September 8, 1958, Archbishop Henry J. O'Brien broke ground for a modern cathedral. The basement of the new structure was blessed by the prelate on February 10, 1961, and on October 3, Auxiliary Bishop John F. Hackett blessed the cornerstone. Auxiliary Bishop John F. Hackett likewise consecrated the completed St. Joseph Cathedral on May 15, 1962. St. Joseph School merged with St. Anne's and St. Peter's in 1987, becoming Cathedral Regional School. In June 2001, Cathedral Regional School closed its doors after educating city schoolchildren for 122 years.

HOLY TRINITY, HARTFORD

Lithuanian
Established 1900
Current Administrator: Father Charles E. Jacobs
200 households

Father Joseph Zebris of St. Andrew Church, New Britain, began to offer Mass for Hartford's Lithuanian immigrants in a rented room on Sheldon Street. In 1900, a plot of land at 41 Capitol Avenue was purchased. Holy Trinity became a parish in September 1903. Vicar General Father John Synnott had dedicated the first floor of a two-story structure on the Capitol Avenue property as the Church of the Holy Trinity on August 18, 1903. The original name of the parish was "the Lithuanian Roman Catholic Church of the Holy Redeemer." Since no additional land was available, in 1913 Father John J. Ambot, who was later named Monsignor, had the two-story brick dwelling moved to the rear of the Capitol Avenue parcel to clear space for a new church. On October 10, 1915, the cornerstone of a new Holy Trinity was blessed. The basement church was completed by Christmas 1915. In 1924, Old St. Joseph Cathedral School at Capitol Avenue and Broad Street was purchased. The school opened as a grammar school in September 1924. The Lithuanian Franciscan Sisters from Pittsburgh, Pennsylvania, came to teach. By the late 1930's, Holy Trinity had become a Catholic high school. With the completion of a new archdiocesan network of high schools in 1961, Holy Trinity High School was forced to close in 1964. In March 1927, the church superstructure was completed and dedicated on March 18, 1928.

OUR LADY OF FATIMA, HARTFORD

Portuguese
Established 1958
Current Pastor: Father Jose D. Silva
1600 households

In the mid-1950's, a number of immigrants from Portugal and the Azores took up residence in the central and western sections of Hartford. The Portuguese population had so increased by 1958 that Archbishop Henry J. O'Brien appointed Father Jose Silva, an immigrant priest, as pastor of a national parish under the protection of Our Lady of Fatima. That year Father Silva purchased a vacant Lutheran church at 170 Russ Street to serve as the first Portuguese Catholic church in Hartford. Our Lady of Fatima parishioners came not only from Hartford but also from many outlying areas, including Newington, where a Portuguese social club thrived. Father Silva purchased property for a church on Kane Street. By 1986, the basement chapel was complete. The new Our Lady of Fatima, an edifice of modern design, was finally dedicated in April 1988 by Archbishop John F. Whealon.

OUR LADY OF SORROWS, HARTFORD

Established 1895
Current Pastor: Father Joseph M. O'Neil, M.S.
Parochial Vicar: Father Francis C. Cooney, M.S.
800 households

By March 1887, about 55 families of German, French, and Irish immigrants in the Parkville area of Hartford were being served by the Cathedral of St. Joseph. Shortly thereafter, Father William A. Harty, cathedral rector, decided to build a mission chapel on Grace Street and launched a fund drive to purchase a lot. On May 30, 1887, the cornerstone of a frame chapel was blessed. On September 19, 1887, Bishop Lawrence S. McMahon dedicated the plain-looking mission. In late 1894, the chapel was placed under the care of the newly arrived French Missionaries of La Salette. On May 23, 1895, Our Lady of Sorrows was made a parish. In 1907, Father Simon Forestier, M.S., built a three- story brick school at 39 Grace Street beside the wooden chapel. It was staffed by the Sisters of St. Joseph. Up the street from the chapel, ground was broken on June 11, 1922, on a small slope at the corner of Grace Street and New Park Avenue. On May 20, 1923, Bishop John J. Nilan blessed the cornerstone of the new church, and later dedicated it on July 26, 1925. Father Cornelius Hayes, M.S., added a second school beside the first. The School was compelled to close in 1992.

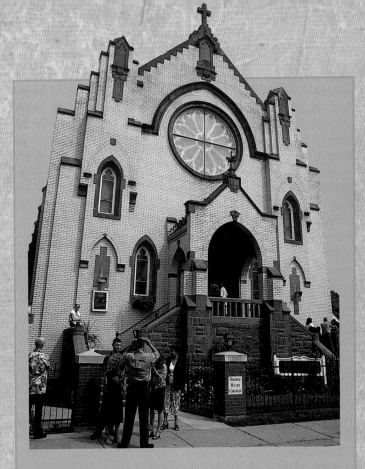

SACRED HEART, HARTFORD

Spanish
Established 1872
Current Pastor: Father David M. McDonald
Parochial Vicar: Father James C. Manship
600 households

In 1829, when the first Catholic parish was organized in Hartford, the city had a sprinkling of German immigrants. On March 8, 1872, Bishop Francis P. McFarland appointed Father Joseph Schaele to care for them. Father Schaele offered the first Mass for Germans on March 31, 1872, at St. Peter School hall. On June 29, 1892, Father Nicholas Schneider broke ground for a church on Ely Street. Bishop Lawrence S. McMahon dedicated the one-story Sacred Heart church on April 9, 1893. Bishop Michael A. Tierney made Sacred Heart a parish in 1897. Father Anthony Kaicher completed construction of the upper church and Bishop John J. Nilan dedicated Sacred Heart on June 17, 1917. In 1955, Father Andrew J. Cooney of St. Peter's, Hartford, opened the San Juan Centro Católico on Albany Avenue to serve Hispanic Catholics who had moved into the area. Soon, the center moved into the basement of Sacred Heart. In the 1970s, the center became a nonprofit corporation and moved to its own headquarters.

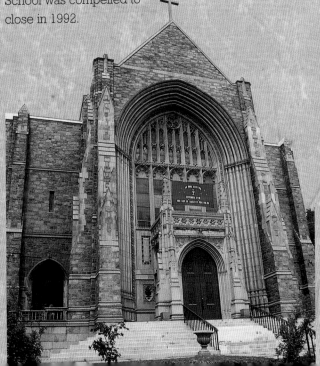

St. Anne-Immaculate Conception, Hartford

Multi-ethnic
Established 2000
Current Pastor: Father James T. Lowery, M.S.
870 households

French Canadians migrated to Hartford with great frequency in the 1880s as local employment prospects broadened. Initially, most immigrants attended St. Joseph Cathedral. In October 1888, French Canadians gathered to plan a national parish. On January 6, 1889, they heard Mass for the first time as a French community at St. Joseph's school hall on Capitol Avenue and Broad Street. The date also marked the canonical establishment of St. Anne Parish by Father Arthur St. Louis. Father Paul-Eugene Roy bought land on the corner of Park and Putnam Street. On December 12, 1891 a wooden church and school was built, the cornerstone being blessed on August 14, 1892 by Bishop McMahon. In the 1920's Father J.V.E. Belanger built the present Church. Father W. Arthur Routhier bought the Lawrence Street School in 1936 and renovated the building as a convent and school, staffed by the Daughters of the Holy Ghost, which opened in the 1940's, as St. Anne School, 176 Babcock St. , Hartford. The school closed in July 1987. The parish of the Immaculate Conception was founded in April 12, 1889 from the Cathedral Parish by order of Bishop Tierney, under Father John T. Winters. This Irish and English speaking Parish welcomed the Spanish community in the 1970's. Immaculate Conception Parish merged with St. Anne's on September 24, 2000, with Bishop Peter Rosazza saying the first Mass in three languages as a new ethnic parish.

St. Augustine, Hartford

Established 1902
Current Pastor: Father Nicholas J. Cesaro
1100 households

In August 1902, Bishop Michael A. Tierney appointed Father Michael Barry founding pastor of the newly established St. Augustine parish. The foundation of a basement chapel was dedicated by Bishop Tierney on February 22, 1903. Until then, Mass was offered at the Washington Street School. Finally, a beautiful Romanesque edifice rose on Campfield Avenue and was dedicated by Bishop John J. Nilan in June 1912. In 1912, during St. Augustine's formative years, Mother Herman Joseph led seven Sisters of St. Joseph of Chambery in providing parish youngsters with religious instruction. In 1927, a school was begun on Clifford Street and dedicated on September 9, 1928. An honor came to the parish on July 23, 1934, when the Hartford City Council named the vicinity of the church Barry Square in tribute to the pastor who had been elevated to domestic prelate in 1933.

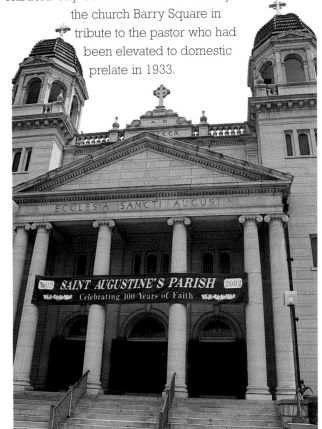

SS. Cyril & Methodius, Hartford

Polish
Established 1902
Current Pastor: Father William P. Przybylo
Parochial Vicar: Father Kazimierz Heisig
2000 households

Prior to 1898, the few Polish immigrants in Hartford attended St. Peter Church. In January 1901, the recently ordained Father Stanislaus Lozowski was assigned as curate to serve the Polish immigrants at St. Peter. On April 6, 1902, Bishop Michael A. Tierney established SS. Cyril and Methodius Parish for Polish immigrants, with Father Lozowski appointed founding pastor. The first parish Mass was celebrated in St. Peter's basement. A small wooden church was dedicated on Governor Street. In September 1905, a parochial school, also on Governor Street, opened to 120 pupils under the Felician Sisters, who lived in the school. Polish Catholics next erected a large brick church. On July 9, 1916, the cornerstone was blessed. Father Stanislaus Musiel then launched a campaign for a new school in 1922. With the school age population expanding, an edifice of 16 classrooms was built on Groton Street and opened on September 6, 1923.

St. Justin, Hartford

Established 1924
Current Pastor: Father David M. McDonald
Parochial Vicar: Father James C. Manship
300 households

In 1914 Father Francis P. Nolan of St. Thomas Seminary, who was Diocesan Director of Cemeteries, built a residence on land that had been the Thomas farm in the Hartford section known as "Blue Hills." On October 16, 1924, the parish of St. Justin was established, with Father Nolan named founding pastor. The site of early Masses was Northwest School on Woodland Street until February 1, 1925, when the basement of a new Blue Hills Avenue church was formally

dedicated. On May 21, 1933, Bishop John J. Nilan dedicated St. Justin. In 1938, Father Nolan purchased land on Cornwall Street for a future parish school. The dream of a school materialized on August 6, 1951, as then Bishop Henry J. O'Brien dedicated the facility constructed by the parish on Blue Hills Avenue staffed by the Sisters of Notre Dame de Namur. The pastor continued the momentum of parochial expansion in November 1961 with an addition to the school of six new classrooms and a gymnasium. The school closed in 1989.

St. Lawrence O'Toole, Hartford

Established 1885
Current Pastor: Father Joseph T. Devine
Parochial Vicar: Father Paul F. Kenefick
500 Households

From 1859 until 1881, the first Catholics of the southwest section of Hartford belonged to St. Peter on Main Street. In the 1870s Catholic numbers had risen to about 400, a fact prompting Father Lawrence Walsh of St. Peter to acquire land at the corner of Wilson and Laurel (later Hillside Avenue) Streets for a church. The new chapel, named for Father Walsh's patron saint, was dedicated on December 3, 1876, by Bishop Thomas Galberry. In 1881, jurisdiction over the mission chapel passed to the Cathedral of St. Joseph. In 1883, St. Lawrence mission was made a parish by Bishop Lawrence S. McMahon, who named Father John F. Lenahan first pastor. Father James J. Smith bought land in 1895 at the corner of Wilson Street and Hillside Avenue for a lyceum building to serve the young people. With encouragement from Bishop John J. Nilan, Father John A. Dooley purchased four lots on New Britain Avenue in February 1926. On April 29, 1928, a solidly built basement chapel was blessed by Bishop Nilan. Father John J. Kelley completed the superstructure of the church, which was dedicated on October 24, 1954, by Archbishop Henry J. O'Brien.

When a fire destroyed the Cathedral of St. Joseph at the end of 1956, St. Lawrence O'Toole Church served as the pro-cathedral for the Archdiocese until the new cathedral was constructed.

St. Luke, Hartford

Established 1930
Current Pastor: Father Frederick M. Aniello
200 households

St. Luke parish was created on June 5, 1930, by Bishop John J. Nilan, who appointed Father Walter Casey as founding pastor. Father Casey soon visited the nearby Dr. James Naylor School which would serve temporarily for Sunday Mass. Property was soon purchased for future church construction. The parish environs were being heavily settled by Italians. St. Luke basement church was constructed on Eaton Street and dedicated by Auxiliary Bishop Maurice F. McAuliffe on July 12, 1931. Father Francis J. Reardon soon announced a fund drive to build a new church on the Bolton Street site of the St. Luke church hall. Before the edifice could be demolished, however, a fire of unknown origin destroyed it in July 1965. Church construction proceeded, and on July 17, 1966, the modern St. Luke Church was dedicated by Archbishop Henry J. O'Brien.

St. Michael, Hartford

Established 1900
Current Pastor: Father David M. McDonald
Parochial Vicar: Father James C. Manship
500 households

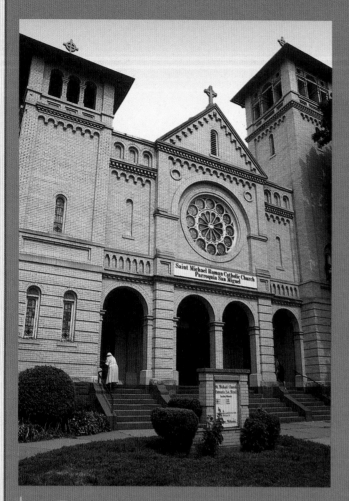

Bishop Henry J. O'Brien to establish a center for African-American Catholics on North Main Street in Hartford. The result was the establishment of St. Benedict Center on March 5, 1948. In 1962, the Archdiocese closed St. Benedict Center, and parishoners merged with St. Michael parish. The parish school closed in the early 1970s.

St. Michael parish was created out of a northern portion of Hartford's St. Patrick parish in 1900. In January 1900, the Diocese had purchased land from the estate of Timothy Steele on Clark Street as a future church site. In May of that year, the church foundation was excavated, and on Sunday, July 1, Bishop Michael A. Tierney blessed the cornerstone. On September 2, 1900, the basement chapel was dedicated by Bishop Tierney. Father John J. Downey was appointed first pastor of St. Michael on October 28, 1900. On June 24, 1906, the upper portion of St. Michael Church was dedicated by Bishop Tierney. On June 4, 1927, the cornerstone of St. Michael School was blessed, and Bishop John J. Nilan dedicated the building on September 11, 1928, to be staffed by the Sisters of Mercy. In 1945, Fathers John Laughlin and Robert D. McGrath of St. Thomas Seminary had petitioned then

St. Patrick-St. Anthony, Hartford

Established 1829
Current Pastor: Father James F. Hynes, O.F.M.
Parochial Vicars: Fathers Andrew Giardino, O.F.M. and John Murphy, O.F.M.
900 households

small space also housed the offices of Connecticut's first Catholic newspaper, The Catholic Press. The parish was confirmed as the Mother Church of Connecticut in 1844 following the creation of the new Diocese of Hartford covering both Connecticut and Rhode Island a year earlier.

In 1848 and 1852, Father John Brady, fourth pastor yet a true founding father of Connecticut Catholicism, purchased cemetery plots called Cathedral Cemetery, and a large tract called St. Patrick's Cemetery.

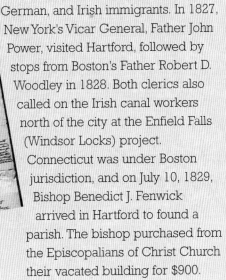

In May 1823, Boston's Bishop John Cheverus said Mass at the Connecticut State House on Main Street for a tiny band of Hartford Catholics, a sprinkling of French, German, and Irish immigrants. In 1827, New York's Vicar General, Father John Power, visited Hartford, followed by stops from Boston's Father Robert D. Woodley in 1828. Both clerics also called on the Irish canal workers north of the city at the Enfield Falls (Windsor Locks) project.

Connecticut was under Boston jurisdiction, and on July 10, 1829, Bishop Benedict J. Fenwick arrived in Hartford to found a parish. The bishop purchased from the Episcopalians of Christ Church their vacated building for $900. The building was moved from the north corner of Main Street to a lot on Talcott Street. Father Bernard O'Cavanaugh was appointed the first resident pastor for Connecticut. On June 17, 1830, the new parish dedicated a renovated structure to the Most Holy and Undivided Trinity, known as Holy Trinity. Before the church was ready for use, Mass was celebrated in a rented room and then in a Masonic Hall.

The first parochial school in Connecticut opened on November 2, 1830, in the basement of the church. The

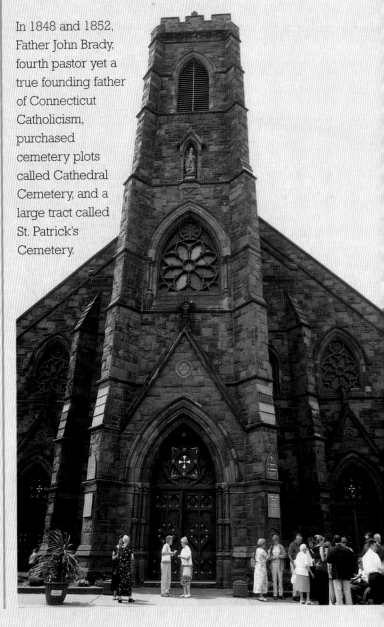

A new brownstone church of Gothic style designed by Patrick Keely was dedicated by Bishop John Fitzpatrick of Boston on December 14, 1851. It was at this time under Father Brady that the name was changed to St. Patrick. In 1852, the first religious community of sisters in Connecticut, the Sisters of Mercy, were brought to Hartford to staff the parish school. Besides caring for orphan girls, in September 1852 the sisters opened St. Catherine's Academy, a private school for young women. Only two years later in May,

Father John Brady

a mysterious fire attributed to the emerging Hartford Know-Nothings destroyed Holy Trinity Church on Talcott Street, and with it the baptismal register dating from 1829. In 1855, Father James Hughes established St. James Orphanage for boys, a ministry originating with Father Brady. In 1865, a new three-story brick school was erected on Allyn Street. A year later, the services of the Christian Brothers were secured to monitor boys' education, ending the use of lay teachers since the founding of the parish school in 1830.

In the early morning hours of January 24, 1875, St. Patrick's Church was destroyed by fire of suspicious origin. While a new church was begun, Mass was held at nearby Allyn Hall on the corner of Asylum and Trumbull Streets, the present site of the Hartford Civic Center. On January 23, 1876, the basement chapel of the new St. Patrick's Church, once again designed by Patrick Keely, was dedicated. The completed church was later dedicated that November. A spacious new parochial school was erected on Ann Street in 1897, now exclusively under the Sisters of Mercy since the departure of the Christian Brothers in 1885. The building would later be demolished in 1982. During the tenure of Father William Rogers, St. James Orphanage closed and the remaining orphans were sent to New Haven's St. Francis Orphan Asylum in 1916.

Once again, in the early morning hours of December 30, 1956, a fire of suspicious origin totally gutted the old church. The suspected arson would this time direct the dying parish into a remarkable rebirth. By 1870, about 350 Italians were living in Hartford. After the Civil War, these Italian Catholics were visited by Father Leo Rizzo da Saracena, O.F.M., of Winsted, who offered Mass in St. Patrick's basement. On January 5, 1895, Bishop Michael Tierney appointed Father Edward A. Flannery as pastor of the Hartford Italians. Father Denis Gleason had been renting a brownstone church on Market Street, built in 1854 by the Missionary Society of Christ Episcopal parish. On June 6, 1898, the renovated stone structure was dedicated by Bishop Tierney under the patronage of St. Anthony.

Plans for a new church were discussed in 1920, and three lots on Talcott Street and one on Market Street were purchased. Construction was soon underway, and on October 31, 1921, St. Anthony's basement chapel on Talcott Street was dedicated by Bishop John J. Nilan. The old brownstone church on Market Street was refurbished as a parish hall known as Casa Maria. Father Andrew J. Kelly established the Catholic Lending Library in 1935. A parish school was founded in 1944, staffed by the Religious Teachers Filippini. In 1948, Father Alexis Riccio purchased the Warburton Chapel on Temple Street and renamed it Casa Andrea.

But change soon shook St. Anthony. From 1953 to 1957, urban redevelopment reduced parish numbers as housing was eliminated. The parish plant itself was threatened by plans that included the construction of Constitution Plaza. Consultation with federal, state, and local authorities produced a compromise to save the parish, but the solution later proved unworkable. In 1957, Archbishop Henry J. O'Brien proposed a merger between St. Anthony's, a parish losing its church, and St. Patrick's, a parish losing its parishioners. St. Patrick School closed in the 1960s. In 1958, Archbishop O'Brien dedicated St. Patrick-St. Anthony Church but Father Riccio ably ensured its place as a precedent in Archdiocesan history. Casa Maria, the only building left of the original St. Anthony's parish plant, eventually housed archdiocesan offices, including the Catholic Library and Information Center and The Catholic Bookstore. In 1990, the parish passed to the care of the Franciscan Friars of New York City.

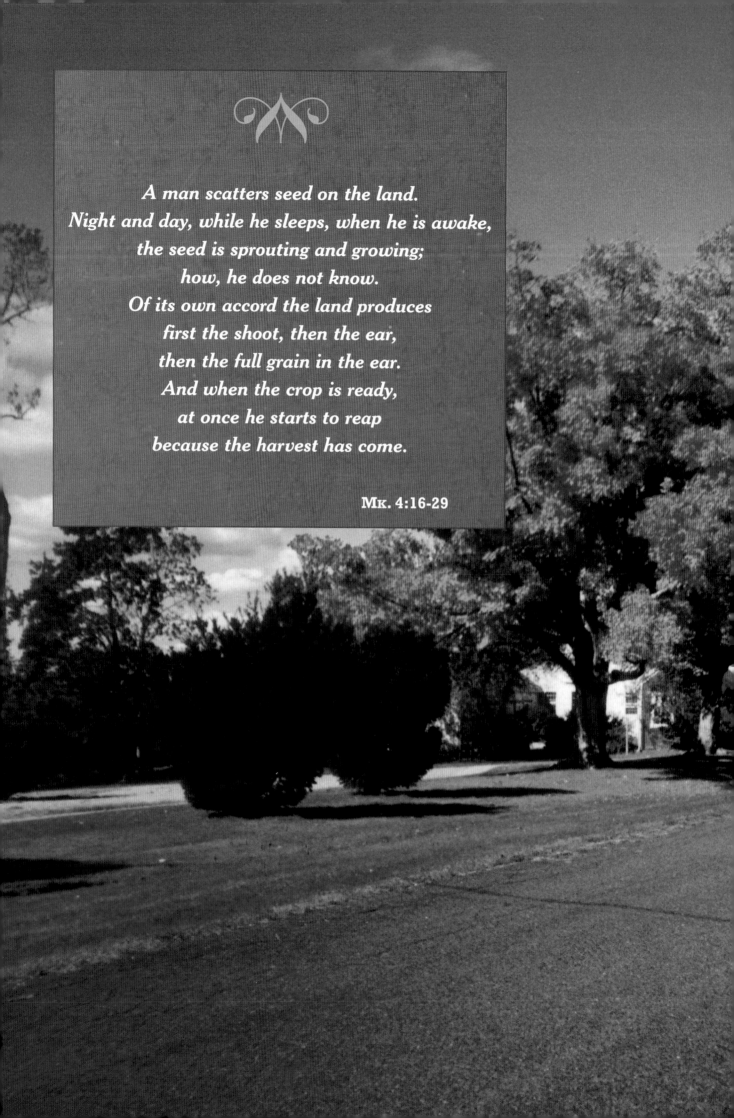

A man scatters seed on the land.
Night and day, while he sleeps, when he is awake,
the seed is sprouting and growing;
how, he does not know.
Of its own accord the land produces
first the shoot, then the ear,
then the full grain in the ear.
And when the crop is ready,
at once he starts to reap
because the harvest has come.

Mк. 4:16-29

St. Peter, Hartford

Established 1859
Current Pastor: Father Michael S. Galasso
200 households

On September 25, 1859, Bishop Francis P. McFarland announced the creation of a new parish, St. Peter. Father Peter Kelly was appointed founding pastor. An old school on the South Green had been purchased on September 7, 1859, for use as St. Peter Church. There Father Kelly first celebrated Mass on October 2, 1859. The pastor's next task was erecting a school behind the church. Initially staffed by lay men and women, St. Peter School opened in 1860 and was actually incorporated into Hartford's public system as the "Main Street Branch," an arrangement that lasted until 1866. A new St. Peter's was erected around the first church on the exact site so that Masses went on as usual throughout construction. On July 26, 1868, Bishop McFarland dedicated the church. More change swept the parish by September 1868, when the school became an exclusively parochial institution operated by the Sisters of Mercy. In addition to the parochial school, the sisters also ran a private academy for girls until 1877. A new school was

built south of the church and dedicated on December 20, 1914. In 1987, the parish school became part of Cathedral Regional School on Farmington Avenue. The school finally closed in June 2001.

Immaculate Heart of Mary, Harwinton

Established 1956
Current Pastor: Father Allan J. Hill
720 households

By 1913, priests from St. Francis of Assisi Parish in Torrington started offering Mass in Harwinton. Torrington priests first celebrated Mass at private homes in Harwinton, then later at Hogan's Hotel and the old academy. By the 1940s, Lou Cronan and his associates secured the use of town hall for Sunday worship, which was first offered there on May 30, 1943, by Father Joseph Flanagan. On October 10, 1944, Bishop Maurice F. McAuliffe authorized St. Francis to buy land for a mission church at the intersections of Routes 4 and 116. Construction got underway, and the first Mass in the newly built mission church was offered by Father Daniel J. Manning on April 3, 1949. Then Bishop Henry J. O'Brien dedicated the white mission church to the Immaculate Heart of Mary on July 3. On September 27, 1956, Immaculate Heart of Mary was made a parish with the appointment of Father John J. Finn as pastor. The need for more space soon impelled the energetic pastor to construct a parish center. On March 20, 1966, excavations began on the parish acreage for a new church and catechetical center. On Christmas Eve 1966, Father Finn celebrated midnight Mass in the new parish Church.

St. Paul, Kensington

Established 1878
Current Pastors: Father Herman Czaster, O.F.M.Conv., Father Herbert Obijiski, O.F.M. Conv.
Parochial Vicars: Fathers Michael Englert, O.F.M.Conv., Marion Tolczyk, O.F.M.Conv.
3100 households

Mass was not available to the Irish families of Kensington until Father Luke Daly of New Britain visited the Berlin area sometime in 1872. The priest celebrated Mass at Hart's Hall on Main Street, Kensington. Father Daly bought property on Main Street in early September 1873. Church construction began, and the cornerstone was blessed on October 27, 1878. Named for St. Paul, the unfinished building was dedicated by Father Hugh Carmody of New Britain in May 1879. St. Paul was designated a full parish by Bishop Lawrence S. McMahon two years later with Father Paul F. McAlenney appointed first pastor. A suspicious fire on March 5, 1913, completely destroyed St. Paul Church. The worship site was relocated to the parish hall. On June 4, 1913, the Condon property at Alling and Peck Streets was purchased as the site of a new church. Construction began and on November 2, 1913, the cornerstone was blessed. A parish junior high school was opened in September 1958. On August 1, 1985, the Franciscan priests assumed charge of the parish.

Sacred Heart, Kent

Established 1970
Current Pastor: Father Thomas E. Berberich
250 households

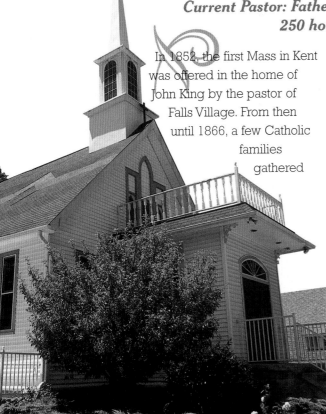

In 1852, the first Mass in Kent was offered in the home of John King by the pastor of Falls Village. From then until 1866, a few Catholic families gathered for worship every three months at the home of Dennis Tobin. Later, Mass was celebrated at a local hall. Beginning in 1871, Kent became a formal mission of New Milford, during which period priests from St. Francis Xavier Parish offered the liturgy at the District School. In 1883, Cornwall Bridge became responsible for Kent's spiritual needs. Father William O'Reilly Sheridan, the pastor of St. Bridget, Cornwall Bridge, built the first church in Kent in 1884 on land purchased four years earlier. In 1895, Kent became a mission of Sharon. Small but spiritually dynamic, Sacred Heart finally attained full parish status on June 12, 1970, when Father Vincent J. Flynn was appointed administrator. In 1987, Sacred Heart purchased a cemetery to complete the parish complex.

St. Mary, Lakeville

Established 1874
Current Pastor: Father Thomas J. Kelly
300 households

A few Irish Catholics settled in Lakeville (Salisbury) sometime in the early 1840's. On July 4, 1849, Father William Howard of Hudson, New York, celebrated Lakeville's first Mass. During its earliest Catholic phase, the section passed through a number of jurisdictions that included Hartford, New Haven, Bridgeport, and Norwalk. In 1850, Lakeville became a mission of neighboring Falls Village. In February 1875, Father Henry J. Lynch responded to the local population shift and relocated the parish seat from Falls Village to Lakeville where he erected St. Mary Church. Father Luke Daly of St. Mary, New Britain, dedicated the Lakeville church on January 16, 1876. Father Lynch opened a school in the church basement. A short-lived school was planned and dedicated on September 5, 1883, staffed by the Sisters of Mercy. St. Mary Cemetery was acquired and dedicated in 1885.

St. Anthony of Padua, Litchfield

Established 1882
Current Pastor: Father Robert F. Tucker
Parochial Vicar: Father Nathaniel Labarda
750 households

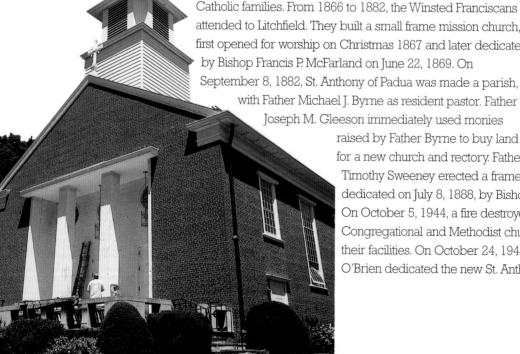

Bridgeport, Waterbury, and then Winsted were given successive pastoral charge over Irish immigrants in Litchfield, yet the first priest to visit the town and offer Mass was Father John Smith of Albany, New York, who came in 1848. Julia Beers purchased a South Street building to use as a mission church for about 140 Catholic families. From 1866 to 1882, the Winsted Franciscans attended to Litchfield. They built a small frame mission church, first opened for worship on Christmas 1867 and later dedicated by Bishop Francis P. McFarland on June 22, 1869. On September 8, 1882, St. Anthony of Padua was made a parish, with Father Michael J. Byrne as resident pastor. Father Joseph M. Gleeson immediately used monies raised by Father Byrne to buy land for a new church and rectory. Father Timothy Sweeney erected a frame church of Gothic style, dedicated on July 8, 1888, by Bishop Lawrence S. McMahon. On October 5, 1944, a fire destroyed St. Anthony Church. The Congregational and Methodist churches immediately offered their facilities. On October 24, 1948, then Bishop Henry J. O'Brien dedicated the new St. Anthony Church.

St. Margaret, Madison

Established 1937
Current Pastor: Monsignor John P. Conte
Parochial Vicar: Father Joseph Keough
2100 households

During the 19th century, New Haven, Chester and Guilford pastors cared for Catholics in Madison. When St. Mary Church in Clinton (now in the Norwich Diocese) was founded in July 1934, Madison became its mission. On Sunday, July 21, Father James J. Kane of St. Mary offered Mass for the first time in Madison's Memorial Town Hall. Worship continued there until a church was built. On March 1, 1937, ground was broken for a church, on a tract purchased in 1916 by Father John Fogarty of St. George Church, Guilford. On August 22, 1937, Bishop Maurice F. McAuliffe blessed the cornerstone of the new church of St. Margaret on Academy Street. On February 27, 1938, Mass was celebrated there for the first time. The edifice, of English Gothic design, was dedicated on July 11. Growth soon resulted in the conferring of full parish status on St. Margaret by then Bishop Henry J. O'Brien in late September 1946. Father Thomas E. Hayes became the first resident pastor, initially residing in a home purchased on the Boston Post Road.

Assumption, Manchester

Established 1955
Current Pastor: Father John F. Brinsmade
1300 households

Assumption parish originated with the vision of Father John J. Loughran, pastor of St. James Church from 1947 to 1949. He first predicted that the rapid growth of Manchester's Catholic population would require the parish to establish a mission. In 1953, Archbishop Henry J. O'Brien authorized the construction of the church building on Adams Street. The Church of the Assumption was dedicated by Archbishop O'Brien on September 19, 1954. Assumption mission was made a parish in June 1955, with Father Joseph E. Farrell appointed first pastor. On October 8, 1961, Auxiliary Bishop John F. Hackett dedicated Assumption School, a five-classroom junior high school on South Adams Street staffed by the Sisters of Charity of Baltic.

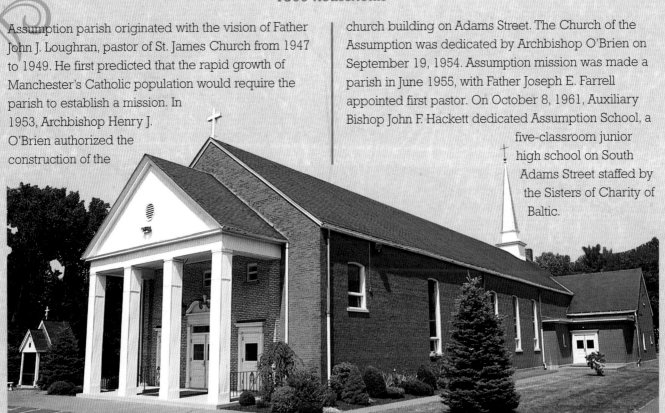

ST. BARTHOLOMEW, MANCHESTER

Established 1958
Current Pastor: Father Thomas A. Sievel
900 households

The territory of St. Bartholomew was carved from St. Bridget and St. James parishes in Manchester. On October 2, 1958, Father Philip J. Hussey was appointed founding pastor by Archbishop Henry J. O'Brien. Father Hussey celebrated the first parish liturgy on October 5 in the Buckley School auditorium. Following a successful fund drive, on June 12, 1961, construction of St. Bartholomew church, school, and convent began. Archbishop O'Brien dedicated all three on May 12, 1962. Starting with grades two through six and staffed by Sisters of the Congregation of Notre Dame, the parish school opened on September 4. By 1970 the school was closed, but the former school building became a thriving center for religious education.

ST. BRIDGET, MANCHESTER

Established 1870
Current Pastor: Father Joseph T. Donnelly
2000 households

Mill worker John Kennedy allowed Father John Brady of Hartford's St. Patrick Church to celebrate Mass in his home in 1848. Visiting Hartford priests also offered Mass at the Union Street residence of James Duffy. By 1854, the Manchester Catholic population numbered 12 Irish families under the care of Father Peter Egan, pastor of St. Bernard parish, Rockville. His successor, Father Bernard Tully, directed the memorable building of a church that was dedicated by Bishop Francis P. McFarland on December 5, 1858. Father James Campbell was named Manchester's first resident pastor in the fall of 1869, when St. Bridget was made a parish. By the turn of the century, a much larger church was needed, and Bishop Michael A. Tierney blessed the new St. Bridget on November 26, 1903. On December 8, 1964, ground was broken for a parish school that would consist of grades 6 through 8. On December 15, 1965, Archbishop O'Brien blessed the cornerstone. The Sisters of Mercy, who staffed the school, departed in 1974 and were succeeded by lay staff.

St. James, Manchester

Established 1874
Current Pastor: Monsignor Douglas P. Clancy
Parochial Vicar: Father Louis D. Cremonie
2000 households

The presence of a silk mill in south Manchester occasioned the need for the town's second Catholic church. An increasing number of Irish immigrants were coming to Manchester for employment. The Cheney brothers, owners of the silk mill, donated a valuable acre of land on Main Street for a Catholic church. The Irish dug out a foundation, and in 1874 the church's cornerstone was blessed. Bishop Thomas Galberry dedicated the imposing building of Victorian Gothic design to St. James on August 20, 1876. But not every Manchester resident shared the Cheney view of welcoming Catholics. The town was the seat of anti-Catholic bigotry in the form of the Orange Lodge, a society comprised of men from Northern Ireland. In

early May 1876, the unfinished St. James Church was vandalized in the early morning hours. St. James received its first resident priest, Father Daniel Haggerty. In 1901, Father William McGurk purchased cemetery land. In 1922, St. James dedicated a brick school and convent on Park Street for the Sisters of Mercy.

St. John Fisher, Marlborough

Established 1972
Current Administrator: Father William L. Traxl
Parochial Vicar: Father Arthur J. Audet
750 households

Beginning in the 1960s, there was a marked growth in the number of Catholics settling in the Marlborough area. Its Catholics had been attending Mass in surrounding towns such as Glastonbury and East Hampton, the latter located in the Norwich Diocese. On June 18, 1972, the mission of St. John Fisher was established with Father Felix H. Maguire as pastor. No archdiocesan mission within memory had begun without a sponsoring mother parish. Later in 1972, however, the mission obtained financial help through low-interest loans from St. Augustine parish, South Glastonbury. Thus, St. John Fisher had adopted a mother parish. At first, Father Maguire celebrated Mass in the basement of Marlborough Manor, a local convalescent home. After state law prevented the continuation of liturgical celebrations at the convalescent home, the liturgy was celebrated at the American Legion Hall. Until St. John Fisher community could erect its own church, Mass was offered regularly at the Grange Hall. St. John Fisher was given parish status in 1974. On May 11, 1975, groundbreaking was held at the scenic Jones Hollow Road tract. The first Mass in the new edifice was celebrated on November 29, 1975. Archbishop John F. Whealon dedicated St. John Fisher on February 15, 1976.

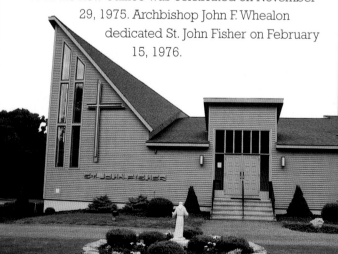

OUR LADY OF MT. CARMEL, MERIDEN

Italian
Established 1894
Current Pastor: Father Joseph V. DiSciacca
1100 households

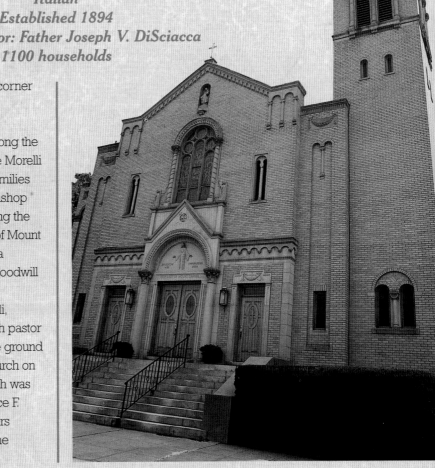

Italian immigrants began settling in the northwest corner of Meriden during the 1870s. The city parishes of St. Laurent and St. Rose initially responded to the newcomers. Sentiment was quickly marshaled among the immigrants to found their own parish. Father Felice Morelli of New York and about 70 families later framed a proposal to Bishop Michael A. Tierney requesting the establishment of Our Lady of Mount Carmel Parish. On May 13, a wooden parish church on Goodwill Avenue was dedicated by Archbishop Francesco Satolli, visiting papal legate. Seventh pastor Father Walter J. Lyddy broke ground for a much-needed new church on May 5, 1935. The new church was dedicated by Bishop Maurice F. McAuliffe on February 16, 1936. The Filippini Sisters staffed a parish school, which opened in 1944 at the former Nathan Hale School on Lewis Avenue.

ST. JOSEPH, MERIDEN

Established 1900
Current Administrator: Father Shawn T. Daly
Parochial Vicar: Father Robert P. Roy
900 households

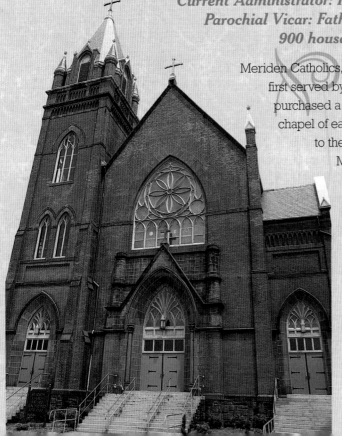

Meriden Catholics, mostly Irish and living west of the railroad tracks, were first served by St. Rose pastors. In 1895, Father Paul McAlenney purchased a former Methodist church on West Main Street for use as a chapel of ease. The ivy covered brick edifice was initially dedicated to the Sacred Heart. On September 23, 1900, however, Bishop Michael A. Tierney created a new parish west of the tracks, under the patronage of St. Joseph. Founding pastor Father John T. Lynch purchased Goodwill Avenue property in September 1901 as a future church site. In 1903, when a basement chapel opened, the old chapel of ease was converted to a school staffed by the Sisters of Mercy. The solemn dedication occurred in early 1908. A new school on the West Main Street Mather property soon enhanced the parish. The institution was dedicated on September 5, 1915, by Bishop John J. Nilan.

ST. LAURENT, MERIDEN

French
Established 1880
Current Pastor: Father Joseph V. DiSciacca
400 households

French and German immigrants to Meriden first attended St. Rose Church. In 1875, French-Canadians were served by Father Thomas Broderick. Meriden's Germans heard the Gospel in their mother tongue only occasionally, during visits by New Haven's Father Joseph Schaele. Responding to immigrant needs, on May 27, 1880, Bishop Lawrence S. McMahon appointed the multilingual Father Alphonse Van Oppen to found a parish for both the French and Germans. These French and Germans heard their first Mass as a combined congregation on June 6 at Grand Army Hall on Colony Street. Father Van Oppen quickly bought property on Camp Street, where groundbreaking ceremonies occurred on July 5, 1880. Bishop McMahon dedicated the church basement, named in his honor, on April 10, 1881. On November 4, 1888, the upper church was dedicated, despite delays caused by the famed Blizzard of 1888. St. Laurent grew with the establishment of a parish school in the church basement in 1893, staffed by the Sisters of the Assumption. In 1903, a new school was erected on Camp Street. It closed in 1998.

ST. MARY, MERIDEN

German
Established 1890
Current Administrator: Father Shawn T. Daly
Parochial Vicar: Father Robert P. Roy
300 households

German Catholics settling in Meriden first attended Mass at St. Rose of Lima. About 400 of these hardy immigrants joined together with French-Canadians in 1880 to establish St. Laurent Church. From the beginning, however, it was understood that the Germans would eventually form a separate worshiping community as their ranks permitted. On December 8, 1889, Germans gathered at St. Laurent basement to plan the organization of St. Mary parish. On March 12, 1890, Bishop Lawrence S. McMahon authorized an independent parish. Having already served the Germans for 19 months as a curate at St. Laurent, Father Ignatius Kost was officially named their first pastor by Bishop McMahon in December 1891. On December 6, 1891, Bishop McMahon dedicated the first St. Mary parish church, a wooden edifice on Church Street. In September 1894, St. Mary School opened with 165 students supervised by a single lay teacher. By 1896, the School Sisters of Notre Dame assumed teaching duties, leaving the parish 90 years later. Relocating the old church to Grove Street, Father Nicholas Schneider inaugurated new church construction. On October 27, 1912, Bishop John J. Nilan blessed the cornerstone. He dedicated the completed Gothic church on October 19, 1913. A new school was dedicated on April 18, 1937, by Bishop Maurice F. McAuliffe.

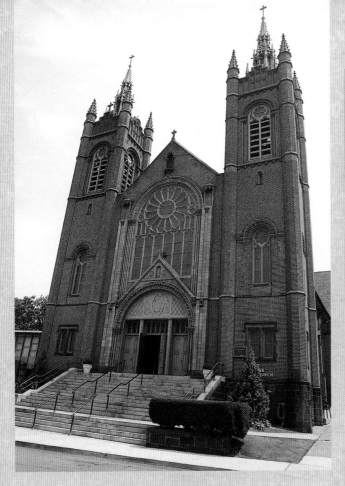

ST. ROSE, MERIDEN

Established 1848
Current Pastor: Father Paul Rotondi, O.F.M.
Parochial Vicar: Father Isaac Calicchio, O.F.M.
900 households

By 1839, Connecticut's mighty undertaking of the New Haven Railroad had drawn in Meriden's original Irish population. The first Meriden Mass was celebrated by Father James Smyth in 1843 or 1844. Liturgies were celebrated in Meriden by Fathers Philip O'Reilly and Bernard Tevin, the latter using the Broad Street home of

Robert Clarke. During the ensuing years, New Haven priests continued to offer Mass in the homes of Meriden's approximately 20 Irish families. On March 31, 1851, St. Rose of Lima was created a parish by Bishop Bernard J. O'Reilly, who named Father Hugh O'Reilly first resident pastor. Father Thomas Quinn convened a school in the church basement, and built a new parish church on Center Street, dedicated on July 31, 1859. In September 1875 a new school opened, staffed by the Sisters of Mercy who left the parish 112 years later. They were replaced for a brief period by the Sisters of Notre Dame.

ST. STANISLAUS, MERIDEN

Polish
Established 1891
Current Pastor: Father Edmund S. Nadolny
1200 households

St. Stanislaus, Meriden, has the distinction of being the first Polish parish founded in the Archdiocese. The initiative was taken by the immigrants themselves on January 1, 1889, when John Damach and friends established a Society of St. Stanislaus, Bishop and Martyr. Liturgies for Poles as a worshiping community were held in the basement of St. Rose church, though the immigrant had earlier attended St. Laurent. With land at Jefferson and Oak Streets already acquired by the immigrants, Bishop Lawrence S. McMahon appointed Father Antoni Klawitter first pastor in 1891. Bishop McMahon dedicated the first St. Stanislaus Church, a small wooden edifice, on January 8, 1893. With a $9000 treasury, Father John L. Ceppa bought land for a new church site at the corner of Pleasant and Olive Streets. The result was the dedication of the new church by Bishop Michael A. Tierney on September 7, 1908. Meanwhile, the old church became the parish school, staffed by the Sisters of St. Joseph of the Third Order of St. Francis beginning in 1914. Bishop John J. Nilan dedicated a new parish school on November 21, 1915.

St. John of the Cross, Middlebury

Established 1904
Current Pastor: Father Thomas J. Barry
1200 households

A few Catholics lived in Middlebury by 1864, as indicated in the baptismal register of Immaculate Conception Church, Waterbury. Though the town became the responsibility of St. John the Evangelist, Watertown, in November 1884, it is thought that no priest visited Middlebury regularly until August 1904. At that point, Father John J. Loftus of St. John's began celebrating Mass at the old town hall. On November 4, 1905, acreage on Whittemore Road was purchased from the Bronson family for $1200. Though the cornerstone of the mission church was blessed on October 4, 1907, the building required another seven years of work. Finally, Bishop John J. Nilan dedicated St. John of the Cross on November 24, 1914. On March 1, 1916, Father William Judge became first pastor as Middlebury finally achieved parish status. The parish included the town of Woodbury, where the pastor lived at first.

Christ the Redeemer, Milford

Established 1966
Current Administrator: Father Daniel H. Connaghan
800 households

On September 18, 1966, Archbishop Henry J. O'Brien created Christ the Redeemer parish, Milford, and appointed Father Richard Toner as founding pastor. He celebrated the first parish Mass at the Mathewson School on September 25. The next year of parish life was highlighted with a building drive for a church, beginning on March 22, 1967. Father Toner broke ground for the church at the Oronoque Road property on August 18, 1968, and construction began. Finally, Archbishop John F. Whealon dedicated the Church of Christ the Redeemer on December 13, 1969. Contemporary in style with a sanctuary conforming to the liturgical directives of Vatican II, the new church seated about 625.

St. Ann, Milford

Established 1924
Current Pastor: Father Thomas E. Ptaszynski
1200 households

By 1900, Devon's few Catholics were the pastoral responsibility of St. Mary Church, Milford. Father Peter H. McLean celebrated the first Mass in Devon Auditorium for about 156 people. On January 14, 1917,

Father McLean blessed St. Ann Mission Chapel, the former Devon Chapel of the local Evangelical Association. St. Mary parish provided funds for the building of a basement church in Devon, dedicated on September 28, 1924. On November 14, St. Ann was created a parish by Bishop John J. Nilan, with Father Edward P. Curran appointed first pastor. St. Ann School, staffed by the Sisters of Mercy, was dedicated by Archbishop Henry J. O'Brien. On April 7, 1962, the ongoing building program concluded with the dedication of a modern brick church. In the late 1970s the Sisters departed and the school was staffed by lay teachers.

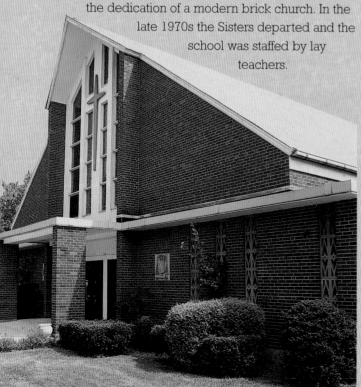

St. Gabriel, Milford

Established 1946
Current Pastor: Father Maurice J. Maroney
1300 households

Catholics in the Walnut Beach area were originally the mission responsibility of St. Mary parish, Milford. Liturgies were being celebrated in Union Chapel by the summer of 1908. Father Peter H. McLean, St. Mary pastor, then erected a Walnut Beach mission chapel, which was dedicated on August 21, 1910. After the original chapel was destroyed by fire in February 1923, a new mission church was dedicated on August 26, 1923, by Auxiliary Bishop John G. Murray. About a year later, St. Gabriel became a mission of newly created St. Ann parish, Milford. On May 11, 1946, Father Robert Sullivan was appointed first pastor of the parish of St. Gabriel. St. Gabriel School was constructed on Tudor Road and dedicated in 1965, staffed by the Sisters of Notre Dame de Namur. At the departure of the Notre Dame community, the Sisters of Mercy served the parish from 1992 to 1993.

St. Mary, Milford

Established 1874
Current Pastor: Father James J. Cronin
Parochial Vicar: Father Ronald P. Zepecki
3000 households

The construction of the New Haven Railroad during the 1840s brought a spiraling number of Irish families to Milford. In the absence of a Catholic church, these immigrants often walked to New Haven's St. Mary church for Sunday Mass. In 1850, Father Edward O'Brien received permission from Bishop Bernard O'Reilly to offer Mass in Milford. On October 24, 1853, the first Catholic Church in Milford was dedicated on Gulf Street. For almost three decades, New Haven and Bridgeport pastors alternated in the spiritual care of Milford, until 1878 when Father Peter M. Kennedy of Derby assumed responsibility. In 1881, a larger church was built at the corner of New Haven Avenue and Gulf Street and dedicated on June 25, 1882, by Bishop Lawrence S. McMahon. In 1885 Bishop McMahon established St. Mary as a separate parish, with Father James Larkin as resident pastor. During the pastorate of Father Dennis F. Moran, Milford's Catholic population rose steadily to justify the construction of a new house of worship. The modern day Gothic Church's cornerstone was blessed on October 30, 1955, by Archbishop Henry J. O'Brien. Spurred on by constant population growth, further parish development proceeded as work commenced on a parochial school, dedicated on June 17, 1961, and staffed by the Sisters of Mercy.

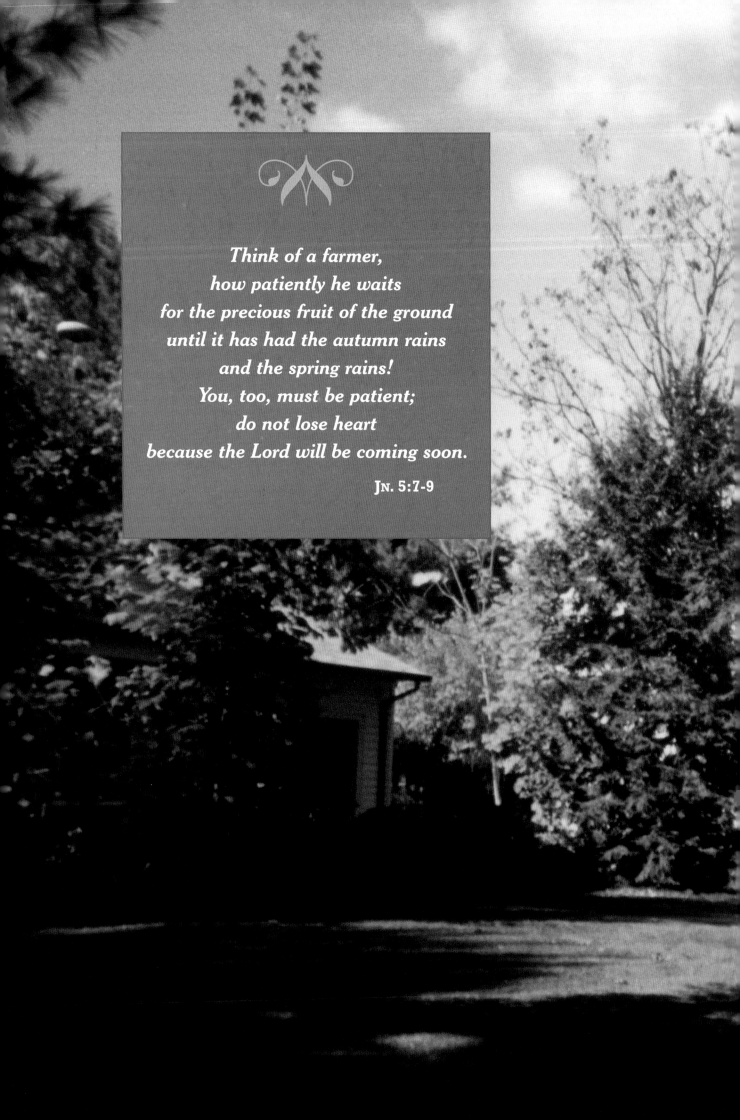

Think of a farmer,
how patiently he waits
for the precious fruit of the ground
until it has had the autumn rains
and the spring rains!
You, too, must be patient;
do not lose heart
because the Lord will be coming soon.

Jn. 5:7-9

St. Francis, Naugatuck

Established 1866
Current Pastor: Father William J. Brenza
Parochial Vicar: Father Faron Columba
1900 households

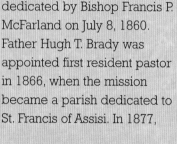

New Haven pastors assumed spiritual responsibility for the growing numbers of Irish Catholics in the Naugatuck area, then called Salem Bridge. In 1847, Waterbury pastor Father Michael O'Neil began visiting Naugatuck to offer Mass at private homes as well as the Naugatuck Hotel. The town soon passed to the care of Derby priests, but reverted again to Waterbury in 1859. Local men bought Water Street property for a church site, which they deeded to the Diocese. At first named for St. Anne, the Naugatuck church was dedicated by Bishop Francis P. McFarland on July 8, 1860. Father Hugh T. Brady was appointed first resident pastor in 1866, when the mission became a parish dedicated to St. Francis of Assisi. In 1877,

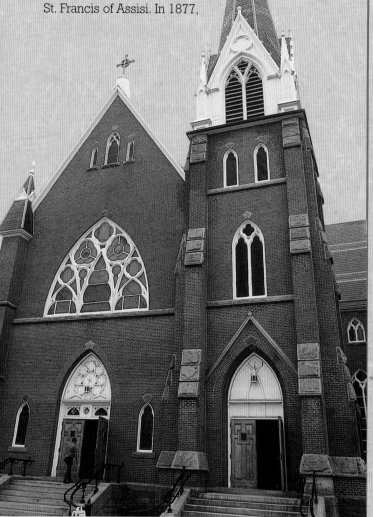

Father Fagan proclaimed a campaign for a new church, to be built on property included in a recent purchase. The St. Francis basement chapel was dedicated on August 26, 1883, by Bishop McMahon. On November 30, 1890, the completed Gothic church was dedicated. On September 10, 1899, St. Francis School cornerstone was blessed by Bishop Michael A. Tierney. A year later, the three-story brick school was dedicated, staffed by the Sisters of Mercy. Monsignor Joseph A. Healy purchased the extensive Whittemore tract on Church Street that eventually served as the parish fair grounds when plans for a more spacious school did not materialize. Sisters of the Congregation of Notre Dame, who succeeded the Sisters of Mercy, were in turn succeeded by the Sisters of Charity in 1985.

St. Vincent Ferrer, Naugatuck

Established 1975
Current Pastor: Father Jeremiah N. Murasso
1000 households

On July 1, 1971, Father Albert Karalis was assigned by Archbishop John F. Whealon to St. Francis of Assisi Church, Naugatuck, with the mandate to develop a mission dedicated to St. Vincent Ferrer. Father Karalis arranged to offer the initial Mass in the Knights of Columbus hall on July 24. Shortly thereafter, liturgies were relocated to the Cross Street School. A New Haven Road tract of land was purchased for construction of a church. On Christmas Day 1975, St. Vincent was made a full parish. Father Vito C. DeCarolis undertook the building of a modern church complex on New Haven Road. Archbishop Whealon dedicated the plant on November 20, 1983. A primary school was opened in the mid 1980s, which later merged with St. Hedwig School, Union City.

Holy Cross, New Britain

Polish
Established 1927
Current Pastor: Father Peter S. Sobiecki
Parochial Vicar: Father Edward Ziemnicki
1700 households

Membership in New Britain's original Polish parish, Sacred Heart, had risen to about 9000 when a movement for a second parish was sponsored by the Holy Trinity Society, founded on April 8, 1927. On November 3, 1927, Bishop Nilan authorized Father Stephen Bartkowksi to organize a parish. To avoid confusion with another New Britain church, the intended name of the new parish was changed from Holy Trinity to Holy Cross. The first Mass was offered on November 13 at a local hall. Father Bartkowski broke ground for a new church on Farmington Avenue on December 29, 1927. A year later, Father Bartkowski offered the first Mass in the new wooden church, which was dedicated on July 11 by Auxiliary Bishop Maurice F. McAuliffe. So many Poles soon crossed over from Sacred Heart that Bishop John J. Nilan recognized Holy Cross as a national instead of a territorial parish, as originally planned. Within a short time, a new basement church was dedicated on July 7, 1935, and Bishop Maurice McAuliffe dedicated the superstructure on September 13, 1942. On August 1, 1954, the long awaited parish school was blessed. It was staffed by the Sisters of St. Joseph of the Third Order of St. Francis.

SACRED HEART, NEW BRITAIN

Polish
Established 1894
Current Pastor: Father Paul P. Wysocki
2500 households

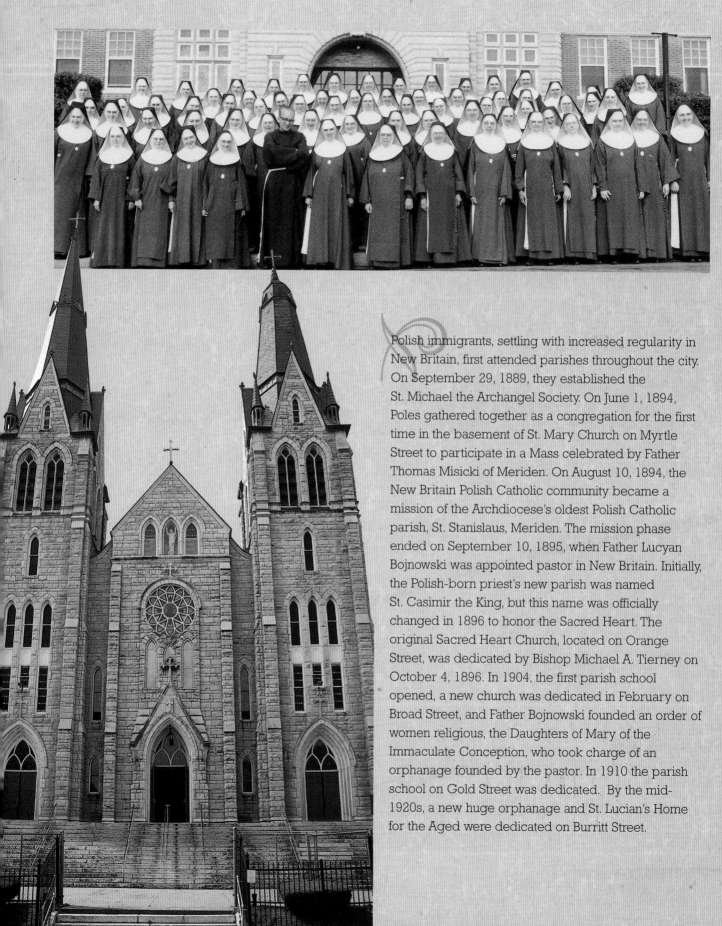

Polish immigrants, settling with increased regularity in New Britain, first attended parishes throughout the city. On September 29, 1889, they established the St. Michael the Archangel Society. On June 1, 1894, Poles gathered together as a congregation for the first time in the basement of St. Mary Church on Myrtle Street to participate in a Mass celebrated by Father Thomas Misicki of Meriden. On August 10, 1894, the New Britain Polish Catholic community became a mission of the Archdiocese's oldest Polish Catholic parish, St. Stanislaus, Meriden. The mission phase ended on September 10, 1895, when Father Lucyan Bojnowski was appointed pastor in New Britain. Initially, the Polish-born priest's new parish was named St. Casimir the King, but this name was officially changed in 1896 to honor the Sacred Heart. The original Sacred Heart Church, located on Orange Street, was dedicated by Bishop Michael A. Tierney on October 4, 1896. In 1904, the first parish school opened, a new church was dedicated in February on Broad Street, and Father Bojnowski founded an order of women religious, the Daughters of Mary of the Immaculate Conception, who took charge of an orphanage founded by the pastor. In 1910 the parish school on Gold Street was dedicated. By the mid-1920s, a new huge orphanage and St. Lucian's Home for the Aged were dedicated on Burritt Street.

ST. ANDREW, NEW BRITAIN

Lithuanian
Established 1895
Current Administrator: Father Ronald T. Smith
300 households

By 1889, New Britain's Lithuanian immigrants, who attended St. Mary's, were numerous enough to plan a parish. By 1893, Father Joseph Zebris was traveling to New Britain from Waterbury's St. Joseph parish, offering Mass in St. Mary's basement In 1895, land was purchased at Church and Stanley Streets for a new church and Father Zebris was appointed pastor. On January 1, 1896, the cornerstone of St. Andrew Church was blessed by Bishop Michael A. Tierney. In 1911, a new brick Romanesque church was built, resting where the first church had been before its removal to the rear for brief use as a school. A friendship and recreation center was established in the remaining part of the old church at the rear of the property.

ST. ANN, NEW BRITAIN

Italian
Established 1938
Current Pastor: Father Christopher M. Tiano
1200 households

An increasing number of Italian immigrants began to populate the cities of Connecticut in the early decades of the 20th century. In New Britain, St. Mary parish began to offer Sunday liturgy with an Italian sermon on February 16, 1908. A signal event occurred in 1932 when Italians at St. Mary formed the Italian Roman Catholic Society. Shortly thereafter, the organization purchased land for a new church and conveyed it to the Diocese of Hartford. On June 3, 1938, Father John B. Malley was designated first pastor of St. Ann parish by Bishop Maurice F. McAuliffe. A basement chapel on Clark Street had been dedicated by May. Work on the superstructure of the church began in 1941 and on April 26, 1942, Bishop McAuliffe dedicated the completed edifice. In 1965, a school opened on North Street under the care of the Filippini Sisters, who came to the parish in 1946. In 1977, the parish school was converted into a junior high school. The school closed in the mid-1990's.

ST. FRANCIS OF ASSISI, NEW BRITAIN

Established 1941
Current Pastor: Father Paul R. Guido, O.F.M.
Parochial Vicar: Father Richard J. Donovan, O.F.M.
800 households

St. Francis of Assisi parish was established in the Belvedere section of New Britain by Bishop Maurice F. McAuliffe in 1941, with Father James K. Brophy appointed first pastor. For a year until a basement chapel on Stanley Street was completed, the pastor offered Mass in the Stanley School auditorium. Archbishop Henry J. O'Brien dedicated the completed church on June 2, 1957. In 1962, an ambitious building fund campaign resulted in the construction of a parish school on Pendleton Road. A year later, St. Francis Junior High School was dedicated and staffed by the School Sisters of Notre Dame.

ST. JEROME, NEW BRITAIN

Established 1958
Current Pastor: Father Thomas J. Cieslikowski
1000 households

In late 1957, the Archdiocese purchased three acres of land in New Britain at the corner of Horse Plain Road and Corbin Avenue. The priests of St. Mary began to offer Mass at the Thomas Jefferson and Slater Road Schools. On May 26, 1958, Father James P. Cunningham was appointed pastor of St. Jerome, a parish officially created by Archbishop Henry J. O'Brien on July 3. On July 6, Father Cunningham offered

Sunday Mass for the first time at the two public schools. By now a 10-acre tract on Slater Road appeared better suited as a church site. Groundbreaking took place on October 16, 1960, with Monsignor Thomas Greylish officiating. St. Jerome Church and parish hall were dedicated on January 21, 1962, by Archbishop O'Brien.

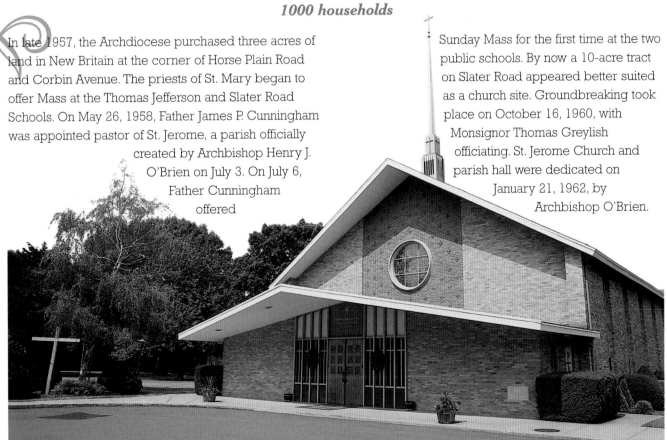

ST. JOHN THE EVANGELIST, NEW BRITAIN

Established 1916
Current Pastor: Father Ronald T. Smith
500 households

St. John the Evangelist parish was established on September 9, 1916, with Father John J. Fitzgerald appointed first pastor by Bishop John J. Nilan. Bishop Nilan dedicated the church, originally designed as a school building, on April 29, 1917. Until the church was ready, parishioners had attended Mass in the basement of nearby St. Andrew Church. On December 30, 1921, the church was partially consumed by fire. Although repairs were made, the goal of building a new church occupied the congregation's attention. In 1957, a piece of property at the corner of East Street and Newington Avenue was purchased from the McGrail family. Prospects for a new church neared, rekindled by the parish golden jubilee. Construction began in 1968. Soon the old church was demolished. The first Mass in the modern brick church on the East Street and Newington Avenue site was celebrated in November 1969. It was later dedicated by Archbishop John F. Whealon.

ST. JOSEPH, NEW BRITAIN

Established 1896
Current Pastor: Father Thomas F. Gaffney
1000 households

Bishop Michael A. Tierney established St. Joseph as a new south end parish on April 9, 1896, appointing Father Richard Moore first pastor. Ten days after his appointment, the pastor offered the first parish Mass in the basement of St. Peter Church. A July groundbreaking on South Main Street acreage preceded the blessing of the church cornerstone by Bishop Tierney on November 1, 1896. On September 19, 1897, St. Joseph Church was dedicated by Bishop Tierney. Four classrooms awaiting a student body had been built on the second floor of St. Joseph Church. On September 9, St. Joseph parochial school opened, staffed by the Sisters of Charity. Later, in 1908, the Sisters of St. Joseph of Chambery arrived to staff the school. Ardent in the service of Catholic education, Father John F. Donohue built a new school on Edson Street, dedicated on November 22, 1931. Seven years later, Father Paul Keating established St. Joseph Junior High School.

St. Mary, New Britain

Established 1848
Current Administrator: Father Kevin J. Forsyth
500 households

In July 1842, Father John Brady of Hartford celebrated the first Mass in town at the Foley home. Subsequently, Father Edmund Murphy of Boston provided ministry in New Britain for about eight months, offering Sunday liturgies in local homes. On September 17, 1848, Father Luke Daly of St. Patrick, Hartford, was appointed pastor for New Britain. In September 1850, Father Daly started building a brick church of English Gothic style on a Myrtle Street lot. Solemn dedication took place on August 11, 1853. By now, the pastor had purchased a four-acre parcel on Dublin Hill for a parish cemetery. In 1862, Father Daly opened St. Mary parochial school in the church and purchased a two-story building beside the church to serve as the school. In 1882, Father Hugh Carmody bought the Lee property on Main Street as the site of a new church. On June 27, 1886, Bishop Lawrence S. McMahon blessed the cornerstone of the new St. Mary church. The finished church of Portland brownstone was dedicated on March 4, 1894, by Bishop Michael A. Tierney. Sadly, a midnight fire destroyed St. Mary Church on January 22, 1902, leaving only the walls standing. A new church superstructure was dedicated on February 2, 1908, by Bishop Tierney. Historic St. Mary School, the oldest parochial institution in New Britain, closed in 1972.

St. Maurice, New Britain

Established 1946
Current Pastor: Father Joseph V. Napolitano
600 households

St. Maurice parish, New Britain, was created by then Bishop Henry J. O'Brien on May 4, 1946, the first new parish of his episcopacy. Founding pastor Father Anthony J. Murphy offered the first parish Mass at Lincoln School on May 12. Father Murphy held daily Mass at a Steele Street dwelling purchased in June 1946 for use as the first parish rectory. Since rapid growth was early anticipated, the parish purchased two large parcels of land facing Steele Street and Wightman Road. Construction commenced after groundbreaking on May 30, 1948. Father Murphy celebrated a solemn Mass on February 20, 1949, at which Bishop O'Brien dedicated the new colonial style church. In 1954, the parish purchased the White Oaks Community Center, remodeling the facility as a parochial junior high school staffed by the Sisters of Notre Dame de Namur. In August 1968, parishioners were saddened by a fire that destroyed St. Maurice School. The institution never reopened. The parochial school ideal lived on, however, through its historical link with St. Thomas Aquinas High School, established by Father Murphy in 1955.

St. Peter, New Britain

German-French
Established 1873
Current Administrator: Father Thomas F. Gaffney
200 households

The first Mass was offered for New Britain's German Catholics in 1872 by Father Henry Wendelschmidt, who traveled from St. Boniface Church, New Haven. The impulse for a separate German parish came from the St. Peter Society, organized in 1884. On July 17, 1889, Father Nicholas F. X. Schneider, a curate at New Britain's St. Mary Parish, was named dual pastor of the New Britain and Hartford Germans. Land was purchased for a church on Franklin Square. Bishop Lawrence S. McMahon blessed St. Peter's cornerstone on November 23, 1890. The following year, on July 19, Vicar General Father James Hughes dedicated the new parish's basement church. The completed edifice was dedicated by Bishop Michael A. Tierney on February 4, 1900. French Canadian immigrants sought membership in the parish at the turn of the century. In 1907, a French St. Ann Society was organized by Father John Guinet, M.S. In 1913, St. Peter was officially

designated by Bishop John J. Nilan to serve the needs of the city's French immigrants.

Immaculate Conception, New Hartford

Established 1869
Current Pastor: Father Timothy A. O'Brien
700 households

The first Mass was celebrated in New Hartford in 1849 by Father Michael O'Neil of Waterbury at the home of John Mangan. Shortly thereafter, Father Luke Daly of New Britain commenced bimonthly pastoral visits. In 1852, Winsted priests assumed spiritual jurisdiction. On December 10, 1856, New Hartford passed to the care of Father Patrick O'Dwyer of Collinsville. Besides private homes, New Hartford Masses had been offered at the Brick Machine Shop, Chapin Hall, Choloe Langston House, and Academy Hall. As Irish and French – Canadians found jobs in the busy local cotton mills, the post Civil War Catholic population witnessed the dedication of Immaculate Conception Church on March 27, 1870, designed by the noted Patrick C. Keely of New York. On August 15, 1881, Immaculate Conception became a parish when Irish-born Father Luke Fitzsimmons became first pastor. The pastor quickly assembled a parish plant that included a cemetery addition (1883) and school (1890), staffed by the Sisters of St. Joseph of Chambery. The school was closed in 1971.

SACRED HEART, NEW HAVEN

Established 1876
Current Administrator: Father James Richardson, S.C.
300 households

Sacred Heart parish, New Haven, was taken from the territory of St. John the Evangelist, whose pastor was Father Hugh Carmody. On October 24, 1874, he bought a former Congregational church on Columbus Avenue, a building that dated as a house of worship since 1852. The refurbished edifice first opened for Catholic Mass on December 20, 1874. On February 14, 1875, Father Stephen P. Sheffrey was named first pastor of the newly consecrated Sacred Heart parish. As his first public act in New Haven, Bishop Michael A. Tierney blessed the cornerstone of Sacred Heart School on April 29, 1894. Dedicated on September 1, 1895, the new school opened to 675 pupils and was staffed by the Sisters of Mercy. In 1990, the Sisters of Mercy left the parish and were succeeded by the Apostles of the Sacred Heart. In 1997, St. Peter's Church and St. John the Evangelist merged with Sacred Heart. As a result of this merger, Sacred Heart/St. Peter School was created.

ST. AEDAN, NEW HAVEN

Established 1900
Co-Pastors: Fathers Joseph H. McCann and Cyriac Maliekal
600 households

In 1872, the town of Westville became a mission of New Haven's St. John the Evangelist Church. Father Hugh Carmody of St. John celebrated the first Mass in Westville at Franklin Hall on Fountain Street. Shortly thereafter, an Emerson Street mission chapel, named for St. Joseph, was erected. It was later dedicated by Bishop Francis P. McFarland. In 1895 Westville became a mission of St. Lawrence parish, West Haven. Numbering about 375 communicants, the Westville mission was made a parish dedicated to St. Joseph on June 10, 1900, with Father John D. Kennedy appointed first pastor. Father John McGivney bought land at Fountain Street and McKinley Avenue for a new church. Bishop John J. Nilan dedicated the sturdy new building to St. Aedan on April 2, 1922. The parish patron had been changed because Westville had become part of New Haven, which already had a church named for St. Joseph. By October 1950, St. Aedan built and opened an elementary school on McKinley Avenue, staffed by the Sisters of Notre Dame de Namur. On October 26, 1957, a bigger school and new convent were dedicated by Archbishop Henry J. O'Brien.

DIVO ANTONIO DICATUM.

ST. ANTHONY, NEW HAVEN

Italian
Established 1904
Current Pastor: Father Joseph G. Moffo, C.S.
400 households

The parish of St. Anthony was established in 1903 by Bishop Michael A. Tierney in response to a surge of Italian immigrants in the Hill section of New Haven. Appointed founding pastor was Scalabrini Father

Bartolomeo Marenchino, C.S. At the corner of Gold Street and Washington Avenue, a beautiful church of Vernacular Renaissance design was dedicated by Bishop Tierney on March 5, 1905. On August 30, 1936, Bishop Maurice F. McAuliffe dedicated St. Anthony School on Gold Street, complete with medical clinic. The school, serving 300 pupils, was staffed by the Missionary Zealatrices of the Sacred Heart, who took up residence at St. Anthony's Home for Orphans. Depressed times and an exodus of parishioners to the suburbs closed St. Anthony School in 1971.

ST. BERNADETTE, NEW HAVEN

Established 1938
Current Pastor: Father Philip Sharkey
1200 households

In October 1914, the Morris Cove section of New Haven was placed under the new St. Vincent de Paul Parish, East Haven. The first Mass in Morris Cove was celebrated on May 29, 1932, at the Nathan Hale School. On July 5, 1934, Bishop Maurice F. McAuliffe blessed the cornerstone of St. Bernadette Church, a brick structure with a seating capacity of 450. Formal dedication occurred on October 20. The Morris Cove mission was made a parish in June 1938, when Father Edward J. Shea was appointed first resident pastor. Another parochial milestone was reached on September 4, 1952, when Father Hewitt welcomed

three Dominican Sisters of the Congregation of St. Catherine of Siena from Fall River, Massachusetts. The St. Bernadette assignment was their congregation's first Connecticut mission. In September 1955, Father Charles Hewitt launched a fund drive to build a parish school. Staffed by the Dominican Sisters, the two-story school was dedicated on August 15, 1957, by Archbishop Henry J. O'Brien.

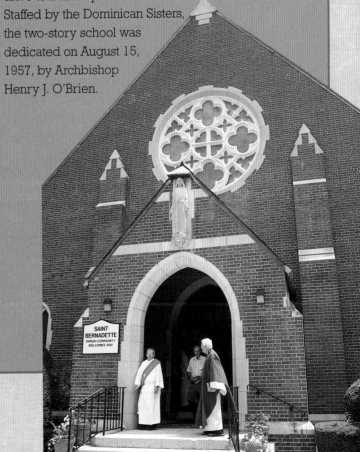

St. Boniface, New Haven

German
Established 1868
Current Pastor: Father John D. Casey
100 households

By 1858, German immigrants met for Mass in the basement of St. Patrick Church on Grand Avenue. Upon the death of the parish's German-speaking curate, the immigrants lacked a priest until July 1868, when Bishop Francis P. McFarland appointed Father Henry H. Wendelschmidt to care for them. Father Wendelschmidt moved the liturgical celebrations first to Arcade Hall on State Street and then to a larger hall on Gregson Alley. On March 5, 1871, 21 parishioners formed the St. Boniface Men's Society. Church construction began, and on May 11, 1873, Bishop McFarland blessed the cornerstone of the first St. Boniface Church on George Street. Father Joseph A. Schaele purchased Germania Hall on Wooster Street in 1893. Within a year, the hall served as both a parish club and a school, staffed by German Franciscan Sisters. The pastor built a more spacious school on Audubon Street in 1908. On June 8, 1923, Auxiliary Bishop John G. Murray blessed the cornerstone of the new church. It was dedicated on June 22, 1924, by Bishop John J. Nilan. By the late 1940s, the Sisters of Notre Dame de Namur had succeeded the German Franciscans in the school, which closed in 1971.

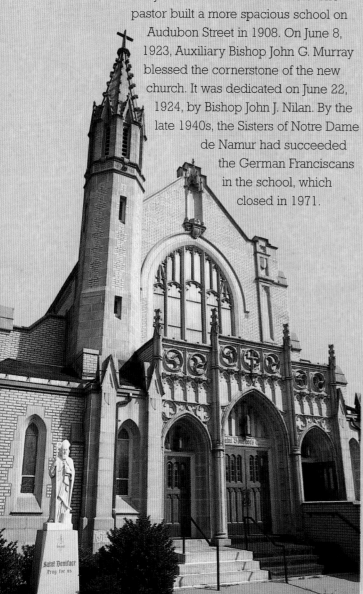

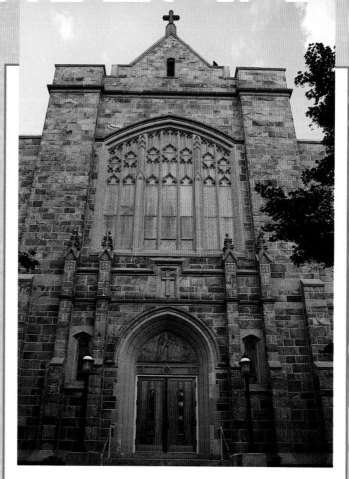

St. Brendan, New Haven

Established 1913
Co-Pastors: Fathers Joseph McCann and
Cyriac Maliekal
300 households

St. Brendan parish was established on April 7, 1913, from the territory of St. Mary, New Haven. Bishop John J. Nilan appointed Father John J. McLaughlin as founding pastor. The priest who had recently worked among Hartford's Italian immigrants opened a frame church on Carmel Street on May 11, 1913, dedicated by Bishop Nilan the following November. The luxurious growth in numbers soon warranted a larger church, and a handsome building of granite was dedicated on January 27, 1924, by Bishop Nilan. Located at the corner of Whalley and Ellsworth Avenues, this scenic site also allowed for the future construction of a compact parish plant. Like that of many pastors, Father McLaughlin's fondest dream was a parish school, a hope finally realized by September 1956. Staffed by the Dominican Sisters, St. Brendan School was dedicated on November 11 of that year by Archbishop Henry J. O'Brien. In 1974, the Sisters of Our Lady of the Garden replaced the Dominicans at the parochial school.

St. Casimir, New Haven

Lithuanian
Established 1912
Current Pastor: Father John D. Casey
100 households

On June 28, 1908, the St. Francis Society, representing the Greater New Haven Lithuanian colony, considered starting a parish. The rising number of New Haven Lithuanians soon prompted the appointment of Father Constantine Szatkus, an assistant at Assumption parish in Ansonia, as circuit pastor to the immigrant colony. Officially assigned on November 3, 1911, Father Szatkus offered the first Masses in St. Boniface Church hall. Before this ministry began, the immigrants celebrated Sunday liturgies in other New Haven area parishes. On August 30, 1912, St. Casimir was canonically established as a national parish with Father Szatkus as first pastor. In 1913, a building on St. John Street was purchased to serve as a church. On January 3, 1928, Father Karkauskas purchased a Congregational church on Columbus Green in the Wooster Street area, which became the new St. Casimir.

St. Donato, New Haven

Italian
Established 1915
Current Administrator:
Father Louis A. Evangelisto
200 households

In 1915, Bishop John J. Nilan recognized the emerging spiritual needs of Italian immigrants in the Fair Haven section of New Haven and appointed Father Charles F. Kelly as their pastor. Fluent in Italian, Father Kelly celebrated the first Masses in the basement of St. Francis Church on Ferry Street. On June 15, 1915, he bought land on Lombard Street as a building site. St. Donato was officially endowed with parish status on December 1, 1915. Open for Mass on December 10, 1916, St. Donato Church was dedicated in early May 1917 by Bishop Nilan.

ST. FRANCIS, NEW HAVEN

Established 1868
Current Pastor: Father Daniel J. McLearen
1000 households

Irish immigrants had been gathering in Fair Haven well before the mid-19th century. Mostly impoverished laborers, they initially celebrated Mass at St. Patrick Church with its pastor, Father Matthew Hart. In 1864, he bought the centrally located Clark property on Ferry Street as a future church site. St. Francis parish was born on October 4, 1868, when Bishop Francis P. McFarland appointed Father Patrick A. Gaynor as first pastor. A basement church was ready for dedication on October 4 to coincide with the pastor's appointment. On August 1, 1869, the congregation, which by now was mounting to 1500 people, witnessed the dedication of their upper church. Father Patrick Mulholland added to the parish plant in 1881 with the opening of a school, the cornerstone of which was blessed by Bishop Lawrence S. McMahon on July 10. The Sisters of Mercy staffed it until 1985. The School Sisters of Notre Dame served in the parish from 1987 to 1988.

ST. JOHN THE BAPTIST, NEW HAVEN

Established 1893
Current Pastor: Father John J. Keane
300 households

St. John the Baptist parish began as a mission of St. Mary, New Haven. In April 1891, it was transferred to Hamden's Our Lady of Mount Carmel. The mission congregation in those early times worshiped in a small wooden building on Alstrum Street in the Highwood section of Hamden. There Father John T. Winters of Our Lady of Mount Carmel offered Mass until 1893, when the Hamden pastor purchased the George Chauncey Rogers property, just south of the intersection of Arch Street and Dixwell Avenue. Soon a frame church was erected on the tract. The cornerstone of the mission church was blessed on July 2, 1893. The formal dedication followed on October 15. On June 10, 1900, the mission reverted to St. Joseph Church (now St. Aedan) in New Haven's Westville section. Father John D. Kennedy of St. Joseph first

administered to Highwood. The prospering mission of St. John the Baptist was made a parish on August 5, 1915, by Bishop John J. Nilan, who appointed Father William Kiernan first pastor. On June 9, 1916, Father Kiernan purchased the Munson property on Dixwell Avenue, breaking ground for a new church in June 1921. Bishop Nilan dedicated the new church on the last Sunday of July 1922. A new school was dedicated on September 24, 1937, staffed by the Sisters of Mercy, who were succeeded by the Congregation of Notre Dame in 1950. Sadly, the parish school closed in 1971. It had been an institution highly respected as one of Connecticut's most racially balanced centers of learning.

St. Joseph, New Haven

Established 1900
Current Pastor: Father John P. Sullivan
200 households

On April 20, 1900, St. Joseph parish, New Haven, was established by Bishop Michael A. Tierney from the territories of St. Mary, St. Patrick and St. Francis parishes. The new and sizable congregation had been ably served from about 1894 at a Lawrence Street chapel of ease erected by St. Mary parish. As the construction of the new St. Joseph Church proceeded on Edwards Street, founding pastor Father Michael J. Daly continued to use the chapel of ease. The land upon which St. Joseph Church was being built had been purchased from the Dominican order, which had planned to erect a house of studies on the plot. St. Joseph's cornerstone was blessed on September 11, 1904, and the handsome Romanesque edifice of brick was dedicated on October 22, 1905.

Ply the sickle,
for the harvest is ripe;
Come and tread
for the winepress is full;
the vats are overflowing.

Jl. 4:13

St. Martin de Porres, New Haven

Established 1942
Current Pastor: Father Joseph M. Elko
300 households

St. Martin de Porres parish grew out of New Haven's Blessed Martin Center. The idea had originated in 1937 when the pastor of St. Brendan, Father John McLaughlin, organized the Blessed Martin de Porres Confraternity at his parish. The society consisted of black Catholics from the Cape Verde Islands. When growth necessitated moving the meetings from St. Brendan to a former Dixwell Avenue police station in 1942, the official name of Blessed Martin de Porres Center was given. Father Peter L. Gerety, later Archbishop of Newark, New Jersey, was appointed pastor. On May 16, 1943, the first Mass was offered at Blessed Martin Center. Bishop Maurice F. McAuliffe presided at the liturgy. The center's chapel was located in the basement. A mission style church was later added to the building. On June 26, 1949, then Bishop Henry J. O'Brien dedicated the church. In 1955, old St. Mary School was purchased. The building became the new Blessed Martin School under the Sisters of Notre Dame de Namur. St. Martin School closed in 1988.

St. Michael, New Haven

Italian
Established 1889
Current Pastor: Father Andrew Brizzolara, C.S.
500 households

St. Michael was created by Bishop Lawrence S. McMahon in response to the influx of Italian immigrants to New Haven. Bishop McMahon had assigned priests to serve the Italians in their temporary places of worship – St. Patrick Hall, the Union Armory, and the Boardman building. Since its foundation the parish has been staffed by The Congregation of The Missionaries of St. Charles/Scalabrinians, founded in 1887 by Blessed John Baptist Scalabrini who visited this church in 1901. Father Vincenzo Astorri, C.S., was assigned as first resident pastor of St. Michael the Archangel

parish, formally established on September 1, 1889. Father Astorri soon bought a former German Lutheran church on Wooster Street. The property was speedily renovated and dedicated in the fall of 1889 under the protection of St. Michael. As New Haven's Italian population increased dramatically, Father Louis Lango, C.S., moved to secure more worship space. He purchased a Baptist church that had been a Congregational meeting house on Wooster Place.

The Apostolic Delegate, Archbishop Sebastiano Martinelli, dedicated the new St. Michael Church on April 23, 1899. In 1936, Father Leonardo Quaglia, C.S., opened a parish school at 125 Green Street, staffed by the Apostles of the Sacred Heart. In 1940 the parish built a separate school at 234 Green Street. In 1966, St. Patrick Church merged with St. Michael church. St. Michael School merged with St. Stanislaus School in 1993. Both closed in 1995.

ST. MARY, NEW HAVEN

Established 1832
Current Pastor: Very Rev. William A. Holt, O.P.
Dominican Friars.
500 households

St. Mary, New Haven, dates back to 1651, when Father Gabriel Druillette,S.J., became the first priest to serve the city. In 1796 a French priest ministered to refugees of the Caribbean. After 1829, when ecclesial jurisdiction passed to Hartford, the Catholic congregation received a resident pastor, Father James McDermott. Five years later, Boston's Bishop Benedict J. Fenwick, dedicated Christ Church, the second Catholic church in Connecticut. In December 1848, a Congregational meeting house was dedicated as St. Mary's by Bishop William Tyler, Connecticut's first bishop, after a fire destroyed the church the previous on June 11. A school and orphanage staffed by the Sisters of Mercy opened in 1851 when ambitious plans for an impressive new church edifice to be located in New Haven's finest residential area were launched. The present church was dedicated 20 years later in 1884. But it was the 1880s that saw St. Mary's influence extend far beyond its parochial boundary. In 1882, assistant pastor, Father Michael J. McGivney, founded the Knights of Columbus, a fraternal benefit society to protect widows and children of working men and foster their faith and social program. Beginning humbly in the church basement with a handful of dedicated men, the Knights have miraculously multiplied to 1.6 million members worldwide.

In preparation for the church's centennial in 1986, between 1981 and 1984,the old church was completely renovated, receiving a new roof, new electrical wiring, a cleaning of the exterior stone, a rosewood floor from Thailand acoustically suited to a grand new organ, life-sized, hand-carved statues, a new floor plan bringing the people closer to the altar and a Carolingian crucifix that replicates one commissioned by the Knights for St. Peter's in Rome. Most conspicuously, a new Gothic bell steeple crowned by an 11-foot Celtic cross now rises 240 feet above the town, its three great bells singing out three times daily. On Founders Day, March 1982, the remains of Father McGivney were re-entombed, making the church a shrine for Knights who visit from all over the world. Today St. Mary's, under the energetic administration of the Dominican Order since 1886, is a thriving church, the primary Catholic presence in downtown New Haven. Its diverse congregation comprises parishioners from steadily aging and often poor old neighborhoods, from new enclaves of urban gentrification and from Yale University's internationalized Catholic community and the Knights. The Dominicans still contribute significantly to its life.

St. Rose of Lima, New Haven

Established 1907
Current Pastor: Father William M. Burbank
500 households

On September 18, 1907, Bishop Michael A. Tierney established St. Rose parish, appointing Father John J. Fitzgerald as founding pastor. Father Fitzgerald celebrated the first parish Mass at Grand Avenue's Polar Star Hall on September 29, 1907. From October 1907 until April 1908, St. Andrew Methodist Episcopal Chapel on Townsend Avenue was leased for Sunday Mass. The basement of St. Francis Church was then employed until a temporary parish church was built on Saltonstall Avenue. The first St. Rose was dedicated on May 10, 1908. Property was acquired for a larger church on Blatchley Avenue, and construction began. On October 6, 1912, the cornerstone was blessed. Bishop John J. Nilan dedicated the new St. Rose on April 20, 1913. A few years later, on September 3, 1916, a new parochial school was blessed, staffed by the Sisters of Mercy. In September a four-room school had opened in a building on the corner of Richard Street and Saltonstall Avenue. The Sisters of Mercy left the parish in 1990.

St. Stanislaus, New Haven

Polish
Established 1901
Current Pastor: Father Waclaw Hlond, C.M.
Parochial Vicars: Fathers Roman Kmiec, C.M., Boleslaw Potomski, C.M.
900 households

The New Haven Polish immigrants in the late 19th century first attended St. Boniface Church. On February 2, 1896, they formed the Society of St. Stanislaus. On September 12, 1900, Father Stanislaus F. Musiel was appointed to New Haven. He celebrated the first Mass on September 16 at St. Boniface Germania Hall on Wooster Street. On December 28, 1901, St. Stanislaus was made a parish. Father Musiel bought property at the corner of Dwight and Edgewood Avenues and refurbished the building for use as a chapel. On January 1, 1904, the parish had passed to the care of the Polish Vincentian Fathers. Father George Glogowski, C.M., bought a former Swedish Lutheran church on St. John Street, which was dedicated as a Catholic church on October 23, 1904, by Bishop Tierney. In 1910 Father Anthony Masurkiewicz C.M., arranged for the Sisters of the Holy Family of Nazareth to teach in a burgeoning church basement school. A new St. Stanislaus Church was dedicated on April 27, 1913. In October 1921, a new parochial school was dedicated on State Street. In 1993, St. Stanislaus School merged with St. Michael's School. Both closed in 1995. The Parish celebrated their 100 th anniversary in 2001.

OUR LADY OF THE LAKES, NEW MILFORD

Established 1990
Current Pastor: Father Frederick M. Langlois
800 households

Our Lady of the Lakes mission was established on March 26, 1989. For the founding 850 families of the mission, it had been a five-mile cross-town trek to the mother church, St. Francis Xavier. On July 23, the new pastor offered the first liturgy for the congregation, a Vigil Mass at Hill and Plain School directly across the street from the rectory, an old farmhouse dating from the 19th century. The chancery had earlier purchased the rectory and five surrounding acres located on Old Town Park Road. On December 8, 1990, Our Lady of the Lakes was made a parish with Father Thomas Ptaszynski appointed first pastor. In 1992, a chapel was built on Old Town Park Road.

ST. FRANCIS XAVIER, NEW MILFORD

Established 1871
Current Pastor: Father Mario F. Julian, O.F.M.
Parochial Vicar: Father Jack W. Hoak, O.F.M.
2000 households

The building of the Housatonic Railroad, in addition to the lumber and tobacco industries, drew in New Milford's first Catholics. In 1839, at a home near the railroad station, New Haven's Father James Smyth celebrated the first Mass in the area. Other Masses followed at the Dunn and Finn homesteads. Though under Bridgeport pastors since 1842, the area was also served by Father John Brady of Hartford. Over the next years, New Milford passed to the respective jurisdictions of Norwalk, Danbury, Falls Village and Newtown. In October 1860, the Newtown pastor bought an Elm Street sawmill and converted it to a chapel. In 1867, a two-acre cemetery plot was purchased. St. Francis Xavier was made a parish on May 21, 1871, with Father Patrick G. McKenna appointed first pastor. Father McKenna erected a new church on the parish property, which was completed and dedicated in 1873. On September 12, 1928, St. Francis School opened at the picturesque Treadwell homestead, staffed by the Franciscan Sisters from Waterbury. Triumphantly, ground for a new church was broken on scenic Old Park Lane on May 10, 1970. The new church of St. Francis Xavier was dedicated on September 11, 1971. The parish school closed in 1973.

HOLY SPIRIT, NEWINGTON

Established 1964
Current Pastor: Father Lawrence R. Bock
Parochial Vicars: Fathers Peter Dwornik, James F. Kinnane
2000 households

Archbishop Henry J. O'Brien established Holy Spirit parish on September 10, 1964, in Newington's southern portion. Father Edward J. Radzevich was appointed first pastor for the congregation of 700 families. In 1963, the chancery had purchased 12 acres of land at 183 Church Street. On this tract of scenic farmland was an older farm dwelling that became a daily chapel. A paramount goal at Holy Spirit was the erection of a church. Sunday Masses were being held at the John Patterson School on Church Street. On Sunday, October 25, 1964, Father Radzevich announced the inauguration of a building fund. The projected parish plant, designed by architect Alfred E. Reinhardt, would include a church, rectory, and parish hall. The pastor broke ground on March 6, 1966. On April 30, 1967, the moment of fulfillment came as Holy Spirit was dedicated by Archbishop O'Brien.

ST. MARY, NEWINGTON

Established 1924
Current Pastor: Father George M. Couturier
Parochial Vicar: Father Michael J. Dolan
1700 households

On July 31, 1919, Newington was made a mission of Father William F. Odell of West Hartford's St. Brigid parish. Prior to 1919, Newington Catholics had to fan out for worship to Hartford and New Britain parishes.

Paper mill owner Thomas Garvan had a prefabricated church built on the site of his own summer residence on Mill Street. Father Odell celebrated the first Mass on June 6, 1920, in the Garvan chapel, dedicated that day to St. Mary. The mission was made a full parish in September 1924, with Father Edward H. Shaughnessy appointed first administrator. The Diocese of Hartford had purchased a half-acre of land on Willard Avenue from parish trustee Peter E. McGuiness on May 22, 1931. With the help of Father Francis Nolan, pastor of Hartford's St. Justin Church, Father James P. Timmons planned and built a Georgian style church on the Williard Avenue parcel. The new St. Mary was dedicated on November 22, 1931, by Bishop John J. Nilan. Nearly five acres of land from the Goodale property were purchased as a future parochial school site. On November 2, 1958, St. Mary School and convent were dedicated by Archbishop Henry J. O'Brien. The Sisters of Notre Dame de Namur assumed teaching duties. On April 2, 1967, Archbishop O'Brien dedicated the new St. Mary Church, which was built on the Willard Avenue McGuiness acreage by Rev. Joseph Buckley.

IMMACULATE CONCEPTION, NORFOLK

Established 1889
Current Pastor: Father John S. Ahern
220 households

It is probable that Boston's Bishop John Cheverus visited Norfolk in 1823 as part of his Connecticut-wide tour. Within the next five years, a Boston priest is said to have stopped in the town. Hartford's Father James Fitton celebrated the town's first Mass for 12 people gathered at the Matthew Ryan home at the corner of Mill Street. Later, Father John Brady of Hartford and other priests continued periodic pastoral visits, offering Mass either at the Ryan homestead or the family woolen mill. In 1850 St. Patrick Parish in Falls Village acquired the Norfolk mission. The Ryan family offered a North Street parcel to Bishop Bernard O'Reilly, who was eager for church construction to begin. Norfolk then passed to the care of Winsted. On December 10, 1865, Immaculate Conception Church was dedicated. On August 10, 1889, Norfolk achieved parish status with the naming of Father Patrick Keating as pastor. Using the original church frame, architect Alfredo Guido Taylor of Norfolk wholly redesigned the church into an Irish-Style Gothic edifice. Mass was held in the Arcanum Building until the totally remodeled Immaculate Conception Church was dedicated on September 22, 1924, by Bishop John J. Nilan.

ST. AUGUSTINE, NORTH BRANFORD

Established 1941
Current Pastor: Father Joseph T. Kaminsky
1500 households

North Branford was an agricultural community with few Catholics until World War I. As the New Haven Trap Rock Company commenced its quarrying in the area, a number of Irish families took jobs, attending Mass in Branford and New Haven. As a formal mission of St. Mary, North Branford Catholics were able to attend Mass at the James Walsh home from 1920 until 1925. Negotiations with the trap rock company yielded Catholics a piece of land. Construction began, and Bishop John J. Nilan dedicated St. Augustine mission church on Route 139 on May 3, 1925. In 1936, St. Augustine became a mission of Guilford. Full status as a parish was conferred by Bishop Maurice F. McAuliffe in September 1941, when Father John J. McCarthy was appointed resident pastor for families of North Branford and neighboring Northford. On acreage donated by Mrs. Daniel Doody, Father Reilly directed the building of a new church, dedicated by Archbishop Henry J. O'Brien on August 11, 1962.

Right
Immaculate Conception, Norfolk

:Gift of the Sunday　　　School Children.

ST. BARNABAS, NORTH HAVEN

Established 1922
Pastor: Father Hugh J. MacDonald
Over 2000 households

The largely Italian immigrant population of North Haven had been served by the pastors of New Haven's St. Francis parish from the late 1860s to the spring of 1891. At that time Father John T. Winters of Our Lady of Mount Carmel parish, Hamden, assumed responsibility for about 23 immigrant families. The Scalabrini fathers of New Haven's St. Michael parish accepted pastoral responsibility for the North Haven Italians in 1908. On October 6, 1920, Bishop John J. Nilan appointed Father Thomas J. Sullivan to organize an Italian parish in North Haven. The chancery purchased land at the corner of Clintonville Road and Washington Avenue for a portable church. Until the church could be built, Father Sullivan celebrated Mass at Memorial Hall. St. Barnabas Church was dedicated on April 16, 1922, by Bishop Nilan. Faced with a congregation that had doubled over the previous few years, he built a new church, dedicated on October 25, 1953, by Archbishop Henry J. O'Brien. Within a decade, a new wing was added to the edifice.

ST. FRANCES CABRINI, NORTH HAVEN

Established 1967
Current Pastor: Father Robert J. St. Martin
1000 households

On September 28, 1967, Archbishop Henry J. O'Brien created St. Frances Cabrini parish, North Haven, and appointed Father Vincent E. Lyddy first pastor. Its territory was taken from St. Barnabas parish. Father Lyddy celebrated the first parish Mass at Temple Street School on October 1, 1967. The Orchard Hill Junior High was later used for Sunday liturgies. In 1968, land on Pond Hill Road was purchased for $54,000. After architects were named, ground was broken for a church and hall on March 8, 1970, as Auxiliary Bishop Joseph F. Donnelly presided. The new plant was solemnly dedicated by Archbishop John F. Whealon in 1971. A Spanish style edifice of wood and stucco, the church could accommodate more than 500. In 1982, a parish center was erected, and a house was refitted as a convent for the newly arrived Sisters of the Sacred Heart of Jesus, who would do catechetical work and run a nursery school.

St. Therese, North Haven

Established 1925
Current Pastor: Father Timothy A. Meehan
Parochial Vicar: Father Alexander J. Cherukarakunnel
1500 households

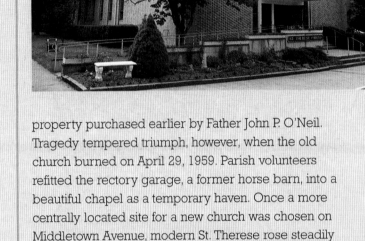

The Montowese section of North Haven attracted Catholics very sparingly. During the late 19th century, the few faithful passed successively to parochial jurisdictions that included Wallingford, Hamden, New Haven, and North Haven. As Montowese Catholics neared 100 in number, Bishop John J. Nilan bought some Quinnipiac Avenue land and built a mission church. On October 25, 1925, Bishop Nilan dedicated the new mission to St. Therese, with Father William J. Daly, appointed administrator. On September 10, 1938,

the mission attained parish status as Father Harold Flanagan became first pastor. Father Thomas F. Dignam began to plan a new church on the D'Agostino

property purchased earlier by Father John P. O'Neil. Tragedy tempered triumph, however, when the old church burned on April 29, 1959. Parish volunteers refitted the rectory garage, a former horse barn, into a beautiful chapel as a temporary haven. Once a more centrally located site for a new church was chosen on Middletown Avenue, modern St. Therese rose steadily and was dedicated at last by Archbishop Henry J. O'Brien on October 22, 1960.

St. Monica, Northford

Established 1964
Current Pastor: Father Joseph Parel
1000 households

St. Monica Church in Northford began as a mission church of St. Augustine Church in North Branford in 1941 before becoming a parish on its own in 1964. During the twenty three years it was a mission church, masses were celebrated first in the living room of Attorney Drugan's house, later at the Northford Community House, still later in the Northford Congregational Church and finally in the chapel of St. Monica built in 1952. The chapel was erected on the land purchased by Bishop John F. Nilan in 1934 and remained the central place of worship for Northford's sixty five catholic families. The population surge in

Northford in the late 1950's paved the way for Archbishop O'Brien to create the parish of St. Monica in September 1964 with Father Steven Vitka the first pastor. The present day church and hall were completed in 1978 at the direction of Archbishop Whealon who believed that the chapel was inadequate for the celebration of the liturgical services for the growing population. The original chapel was then remodeled to accommodate CCD classes, meetings and other parish activities. The dedication and first mass in the new church was held on July 16, 1978.

Under the leadership and guidance of the subsequent pastors Father Stanley Nazzaro (1972-1984), Father John Kaminsky (1984-1994), and Father Joseph Parel (1995-present) the church has grown and continues to be an active, viable institution within the community of Northford with 1035 families registered.

129

St. Mary Magdalen, Oakville

Established 1900
Current Pastor: Father Stuart H. Pinette
1600 households

From 1884 until 1902, Oakville Catholics were the pastoral responsibility of Watertown. When St. Michael became a parish in the Waterville Section of Waterbury, Oakville became its mission. On land donated for church construction by the Oakville Pin Company, St. Mary Magdalen was erected and then dedicated on October 7, 1900. Irish and French-Canadian families formed the infant congregation, given parish status in 1914. Father John A. Conlan was named resident pastor. While a new church was being planned, fire tragically destroyed the old structure on January 25, 1952. Mass was held in the community theater until a new church was dedicated on July 27, 1952. A school was dedicated as a catechetical center on November 16, 1958, and was staffed by the Sisters of Charity of St. Louis.

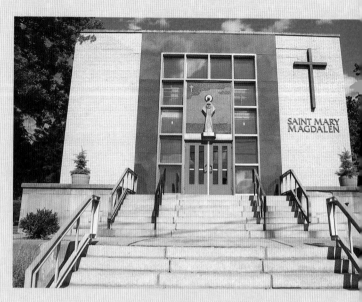

Holy Infant, Orange

Established 1952
Co-Pastors: Fathers Peter S. Dargan and
Bernard D. Killeen
2300 households

Orange had been the responsibility of St. Paul Parish, West Haven. The fruits of faith ripened by 1950 as John T. Gaetano gave five acres of land on Racebrook Road as a church site. Architects were selected to design the future Church of the Holy Infant. On October 21, 1951, the new church was dedicated by Bishop O'Brien. On May 8, 1952, Holy Infant became a parish, with Father Francis T. Monahan appointed pastor. A parochial junior high school, situated on eight acres donated by Mr. Gaetano, opened on September 7, 1966 staffed by the Religious of Christian Education. Times forced the closing of the school in June 1970, but the Racebrook Road complex continued to serve Holy Infant as a parish center.

St. Thomas the Apostle, Oxford

Established 1966
Current Pastor: Father Dominic J. Valla
1200 households

After 1886, Oxford became a mission of St. Augustine, Seymour and then St. Rose, Newtown. Bimonthly Mass was offered at Southford in the Chapel of the Good Shepherd. When a New York City man, Judge Thomas Coman, donated money in 1909 for a chapel, Father George T. Sinnott was able to buy land. On July 2, 1912, Father Sinnott conducted the dedication. Initially named St. Mary, the Oxford chapel was renamed

St. Thomas the Apostle on October 9, 1916. St. Thomas passed to the care of St. Michael Church, Beacon Falls, on November 15, 1924. In 1948, St. Thomas was returned to Seymour's pastors. Finally, after 60 years of shifting mission pastorates, Archbishop Henry J. O'Brien made St. Thomas a parish on September 17, 1966. Father Joseph R. Barlowski became the first resident pastor. On July 20, 1971, parishioners settled on a church site, about three acres on Oxford Road. The Coman chapel was sold in 1972. Archbishop John F. Whealon dedicated the new brick colonial church of St. Thomas the Apostle on January 28, 1973.

Our Lady of Mercy, Plainville

Established 1881
Current Pastor: Father Richard P. McGann
Parochial Vicars: Fathers Edmund K. Karwowski, Sebastian Kochupurkal
2000 households

Since 1848, local immigrant families had been served by Father Luke Daly of New Britain, who offered the first area Mass at the Daniel Kelly homestead in 1851. Beginning in 1864, Plainville was Bristol's mission with Father Michael B. Rodden as traveling pastor. In 1881, Father Paul F. McAlenney was named pastor for both St. Paul's Church, Kensington and Plainville. A new church was built on land at the

corner of Pierce and Broad Streets, a parcel donated by Edward Pierce. The church was formally dedicated as Our Lady of Mercy on September 24, 1882. In February 1885, Our Lady of Mercy was separated from St. Paul's Church, Kensington. On July 12, 1887, Bishop McMahon blessed a six-acre parish cemetery. With Catholic population surging, the parish began to use the Plainville Junior High School for additional Sunday liturgies. A modern church of Georgian design was built and dedicated on December 8, 1957. In 1966, Catholic education became a welcome reality with the dedication of a junior high school on South Canal Street, staffed by the Daughters of the Holy Spirit. The parish school closed in 1989.

MARY OUR QUEEN, PLANTSVILLE

Established 1961
Current Pastor: Father Arthur J. Dupont
1100 households

Mary Our Queen Parish, Plantsville, was created on September 21, 1961, by Archbishop Henry J. O'Brien. Father James J. Sullivan was its first pastor. The first parish liturgy was offered on September 24, 1961, at South End School. This facility was used for liturgies until November 15, 1964, when the parish center was available. The site for the future church complex was a 20-acre tract purchased in 1961 from Mrs. William Smith. Father Sullivan broke ground on December 8, 1963. By November 1964, the parish center was completed and in use for Sunday worship. On Sunday, April 25, 1965, Archbishop O'Brien dedicated the new church. Mary Our Queen had the honor of being the first archdiocesan church built according to the liturgical guidelines of Vatican II.

ST. ALOYSIUS, PLANTSVILLE

Established 1961
Current Pastor: Father John P. Blanchfield
1300 households

St. Aloysius parish in Plantsville was created by Archbishop Henry J. O'Brien on September 21, 1961. Appointed founding pastor was Father Robert J. Chagnon. Sunday Masses were offered in the gymnasium of the middle school, while a daily chapel was set up in Theriault's shopping plaza. Eleven and a half acres of beautiful land on Burritt Street had been purchased earlier by Father William H. Kennedy, pastor at neighboring St. Thomas, Southington. On November 10, Sunday Mass was celebrated in a completed church hall. The church was formally dedicated by Archbishop O'Brien on April 12, 1964. The Diana Road rectory was sold to finance a new rectory that would centralize parish functions at the church site. In 1973, the new rectory was occupied.

ST. JOSEPH, POQUONOCK

Established 1874
Current Pastor: Father Robert B. Vargo
900 households

Hartford pastors first assumed spiritual responsibility of the Poquonock section of Windsor, and Father John Brady celebrated the first Mass at the Conroy home in 1848. In the fall of 1848, Poquonock passed to the care of New Britain priests. In 1852, St. Mary Church, Windsor Locks, assumed charge of Poquonock. Father James Smyth rented Franklin Hall, a former Congregational meetinghouse, for Sunday Masses. At some point prior to 1886, the hall was purchased, relocated to Kearney Street and designated Holy Name Hall. The Poquonock Catholic enclave soon desired a larger church for their growing community. On January 30, 1887, Bishop Lawrence S. McMahon dedicated St. Joseph Church. In August 1892, St. Joseph was made an independent parish, with Father John Fleming named first pastor.

ST. ANTHONY, PROSPECT

Established 1943
Current Administrator: Father Philip J. Cascia
Parochial Vicar: Father Joseph R. DeCarolis
1300 households

In May 1936, Mr. and Mrs. Fred Canales hosted a meeting at their Salem Road home for 28 Catholics. Their findings persuaded Bishop Maurice F. McAuliffe to designate Prospect as a mission of St. Mary's. On July 19, 1936, Father Morrissey celebrated the first mission Mass at the local Grange Hall. By the spring of 1937, Mass was moved to the basement of the Prospect Community School. In the fall, construction began on St. Anthony Chapel on property located on Route 69. Completed by 1938, the chapel was dedicated on September 16, 1939. In June 1943, the next phase of St. Anthony's growth proceeded as the mission became a parish with Father John F. McTeague appointed first pastor. The parish was given its own mission in Bethany. On August 22, 1943, Father McTeague offered the first mission Mass at the State Police Academy. By now, St. Anthony's numbered about 700 families, a seven-fold increase from its early days. Accordingly, ground was broken for a new church and rectory on May 20, 1961, by Auxiliary Bishop John F. Hackett. The church was dedicated on October 20, 1962, by Monsignor Joseph R. Lacy, Chancellor of the Archdiocese, acting for Archbishop Henry J. O'Brien.

ST. ELIZABETH SETON, ROCKY HILL

Established 1985
Current Pastor: Father James A. Shanley
1000 households

St. Elizabeth Seton, Rocky Hill, was the first new Christian community to be created in the Archdiocese in a decade. The Archdiocese had joined with St. James to purchase about eight and a half acres of farmland on Brook Street for a future church and rectory. In early June, members of the mission processed a distance of about a mile to space donated in the neighboring Wiremold Company's warehouse, where a chapel was soon established. The mission band held their first Mass as a worshiping community on June 24, 1984. On September 29, 1985, the mission station was named the mission Church of St. Elizabeth Seton, after the first native-born American saint. By 1987, a new church was soon built on the Brook Street property. On October 13, 1989, the mission became a parish.

ST. JAMES, ROCKY HILL

Established 1880
Current Pastor: Father Thomas B. Shepard
2000 households

Rocky Hill was at first the responsibility of St. Patrick Church, Hartford. The first Mass in the town was offered in 1853 by Father Lawrence Mangan at the home of Michael Kelly. In 1873, Rocky Hill passed to the jurisdiction of East Hartford's St. Mary church. On December 3, 1878, Father John T. McMahon, then pastor of St. Mary, purchased land in Rocky Hill from Ralph N. North. In 1880, the mission at Rocky Hill passed to Father John D. Ryan of Cromwell, who began church construction. Mass was then offered in an upper room of the Center School through the courtesy of the Congregational Ecclesiastical Society. The Rocky Hill mission was dedicated to St. James on January 22, 1882, and the new church on Chapin Street finally opened in 1883. On November 30, 1946, then Bishop Henry J. O'Brien designated St. James a parish, appointing Father Francis P. Heavren as resident pastor. Father Robert J. Shea purchased 15 acres of land on Elm Street, a mile northwest of the original church. By now the Center School auditorium was in use for Sunday Masses. Archbishop O'Brien dedicated both church and rectory on December 3, 1960.

*The Lord is waiting
to be gracious to you.*

Is. 30:18

ST. PATRICK, ROXBURY

Mission of Our Lady of Perpetual Help, Washington Depot
Established 1885
Current Administrator: Father Thomas F. Bennett
200 households

Roxbury was successively affiliated with a number of pastoral jurisdictions in the 19th century, including Bridgeport, Norwalk, Danbury, and Newtown. In 1871, when St. Francis Xavier parish of New Milford assumed the Roxbury mission, the Michael J. Pickett home on Painter Hill Road hosted Masses. As Irish Catholics migrated to Roxbury for work at the local quarries in the 1880s, Father James C. O'Brien began the erection of a mission church on Church Street. In 1885, the wooden church was dedicated to St. Patrick. When Our Lady of Perpetual Help parish was created in 1908, the mission passed to the care of Washington Depot pastors.

GOOD SHEPHERD, SEYMOUR

Established 1967
Current Pastor: Father Edward S. Jaksina
1500 households

A dramatic increase within St. Augustine parish resulted in Archbishop Henry J. O'Brien's establishment of the parish of the Good Shepherd, Seymour, on September 28, 1967. Father Martin T. Keane was appointed first pastor. Initially, the priest celebrated Mass at the Strand Theater on Main Street and then later at the Seymour High School auditorium. On October 22, 1967, a residence at 34 Kathy Drive became the rectory. By the end of December, Good Shepherd parish had purchased 5.4 acres of land on Mountain Road. By spring 1968, a new church was being planned and by 1969, an additional 4.3 acres of land was purchased. On May 17, 1970, Archbishop John F. Whealon formally dedicated the new brick Church of the Good Shepherd.

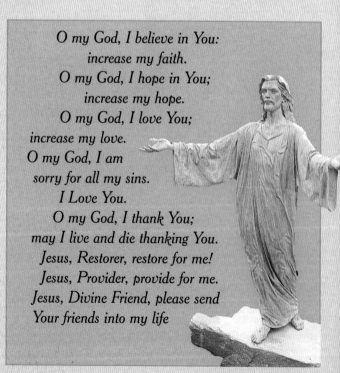

O my God, I believe in You:
increase my faith.
O my God, I hope in You;
increase my hope.
O my God, I love You;
increase my love.
O my God, I am
sorry for all my sins.
I Love You.
O my God, I thank You;
may I live and die thanking You.
Jesus, Restorer, restore for me!
Jesus, Provider, provide for me.
Jesus, Divine Friend, please send
Your friends into my life

St. Augustine, Seymour

Established 1866
Current Pastor: Father Brian E. Jeffries
700 households

In 1844, Father James Smyth of New Haven offered the first Mass at the old Long house on Raymond Street. The building of a railroad in the mid 19th century caused the Catholic population to multiply. In November 1847, Seymour was visited by Father Michael O'Neil of Waterbury. By March 31, 1851, Father James Lynch of Derby was ministering to Seymour. That year, the circuit pastor bought the Blackman land as a church site. In the fall of 1856, a church was completed and dedicated to St. Augustine. In 1870, St. Augustine became a mission of Ansonia. Father John McMahon was named pastor of St. Augustine in October 1885, when the mission was finally elevated to parish status. On July 15, 1888, Bishop Lawrence S. McMahon blessed the cornerstone of a new church designed by noted architect Patrick C. Keely. Formal dedication came on May 18, 1890. In 1957, Father Albert A. Callahan purchased property on Washington Avenue across from the church. At first intended as a convent, the dwelling later became a center for parish religious instruction programs.

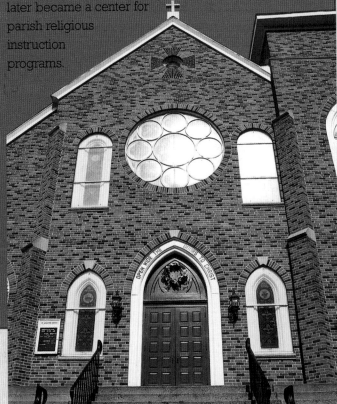

St. Bernard, Sharon

Established 1885
Current Administrator: Father Francis R. Fador
200 households

Northwestern Connecticut's burgeoning iron and charcoal industries began to attract Irish and French immigrants to the Sharon vicinity, which had earlier been under the pastoral jurisdiction of Hartford, New Haven, and Bridgeport. The first Mass in Sharon was celebrated in 1845 for about 30 Irish Catholics at the home of James and Bridget Dunning. Varying accounts identify the celebrant as either Father Peter Kelly of Falls Village or Father Michael Lynch of Bridgeport. A mission church costing $2,400 was built in 1885 by Father William O'Reilly Sheridan, pastor at Cornwall Bridge, under whose jurisdiction Sharon then fell. When the congregation numbered about 450 members, parish status was conferred in January 1896. Father James T. Walsh was named resident pastor and took up quarters in a Main Street rectory. His missions included Cornwall Bridge, Kent, and Warren. The 1912 appointment of Father Andrew J. Plunkett as seventh resident pastor opened a new era at St. Bernard with the completion of a brick church on New Street.

ST. AUGUSTINE, SOUTH GLASTONBURY

Established 1877
Current Pastor: Father Kevin P. Cavanaugh
Parochial Vicar: Father John P. Melnick
900 households

By August 1873, Glastonbury was the pastoral responsibility of St. Mary, East Hartford. Father John A. Mulcahy of St. Mary bought land in South Glastonbury on November 6, 1877 to build a chapel on the north side of Hopewell Road. On April 7, 1878, Bishop Thomas Galberry blessed the cornerstone. The chapel was dedicated to St. Augustine on November 17 of that year. In March 1902, Bishop Michael A. Tierney established rustic St. Augustine as a parish under Father Francis M. Murray. In November 1906, the parish acquired a four-acre plot deeded by the Purtill family that was cleared for a parish cemetery.

ST. MARY, SIMSBURY

Established 1921
Current Pastor: Father William R. Metzler
Parochial Vicar: Father John W. McHugh
1900 households

In the early 19th century, Simsbury was served by Hartford's St. Patrick Church. At mid-century, the town came under New Britain's St. Mary parish. On December 10, 1856, St. Patrick parish in Collinsville assumed responsibility for Simsbury. When St. Bernard in Tariffville was created in 1881, Simsbury's Catholics traveled there. In 1902, as the number of Simsbury Catholics rose to about 300, Bishop Michael A. Tierney organized them as a mission of St. Bernard. Initially, Mass in Simsbury was offered at the town hall. Soon Father Richard Carroll bought property on the north side of Plank Hill Road for Simsbury's first Catholic church. Named for the Immaculate Conception, the wooden church was dedicated on September 27, 1903. The Church of the Immaculate Conception was made a parish on June 17, 1921, with Father John J. Keane appointed first resident pastor. On February 23, 1936, Bishop Maurice F. McAuliffe dedicated a handsome church made of brick on the parish's Hopmeadow Street acreage. During the 1930s, the parish name was changed to St. Mary. The Seven Elms rectory was remodeled as a convent to house 11 Felician sisters who arrived to staff a future school. Father John Weldon bought land north of the convent to build a campus-style parochial school, the first unit of which was dedicated on November 30, 1957.

HOLY ANGELS, SOUTH MERIDEN

Established 1887
Current Pastor: Father Roland M. LaPlante
900 households

New Haven pastors ministered to the Irish laborer families of Meriden until 1851, when St. Rose of Lima parish was established in town. On September 13, 1886, Father Paul McAlenny of St. Rose paid $450 for a land parcel at the corner of Sheffield and New Hanover Avenue in South Meriden, where a mission church would stand. Bishop Lawrence S. McMahon blessed the cornerstone on April 3, 1887. Holy Angels mission church was dedicated the following July 17. Father Richard F. Moore was appointed first resident pastor on January 10, 1888. The tenth pastor, Father Albert G. Healy, implemented the expansionist vision of his predecessor and purchased the Brown farm on Main Street on which a parish center and school were built. The combined facilities were dedicated by Auxiliary Bishop John F. Hackett on April 29, 1962. Holy Angels School was staffed by the Daughters of Mary of the Immaculate Conception and lay teachers. In June 1972, the parish school was closed. A new Church was dedicated by Archbishop John F. Whealon on September 30, 1979.

ST. FRANCIS OF ASSISI, SOUTH WINDSOR

Established 1941
Current Pastor: Monsignor Charles B. Johnson
1400 households

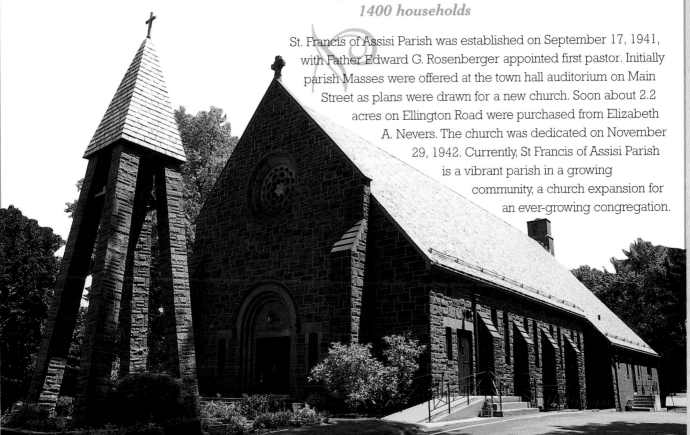

St. Francis of Assisi Parish was established on September 17, 1941, with Father Edward G. Rosenberger appointed first pastor. Initially parish Masses were offered at the town hall auditorium on Main Street as plans were drawn for a new church. Soon about 2.2 acres on Ellington Road were purchased from Elizabeth A. Nevers. The church was dedicated on November 29, 1942. Currently, St Francis of Assisi Parish is a vibrant parish in a growing community, a church expansion for an ever-growing congregation.

St. Margaret Mary, South Windsor

Established 1961
Current Pastor: Father Daniel J. Sullivan
2100 households

The increasing Catholic population in the Wapping section of South Windsor resulted in the creation of a new parish from the territory of St. Francis of Assisi. On September 14, 1961, Archbishop Henry J. O'Brien established St. Margaret Mary and appointed Father Thomas C. O'Neil as founding pastor. St. Francis had by now bought a 16-acre parcel of land for the daughter parish. On September 24, Father O'Neil offered the first parish Mass at the Wapping School. Daily Mass was soon celebrated in the chapel addition to the Hayes Road rectory. On September 21, 1963, Archbishop O'Brien dedicated St. Margaret Mary Church and rectory.

Sacred Heart, Southbury

Established 1884
Current Pastor: Father Mark F. Flynn
2000 households

In 1862, the David Grant home, at Main Street North and Route 67 in the White Oak section of town, hosted a liturgy with Father James Bohen of Watertown as celebrant. Later, Masses for Southbury people were offered at the town railroad station on Depot Hill Road or in Woodbury's old town hall. For nearly four decades, pastors from Waterbury, Derby, Naugatuck and New Milford, had tended Southbury. Father James C. O'Brien of St. Francis Xavier Church, New Milford, initiated the building of the first Sacred Heart Church, a small white clapboard edifice on a hilly plot overlooking Route 6. The site was donated by Dennis Hunihan. Formal dedication, however, did not come until May 10, 1885. The Sacred Heart mission soon passed to

Seymour and then reverted to Watertown. In 1890 Sacred Heart became the responsibility of St. Rose, Newtown. On October 17, 1940, Sacred Heart was made a parish by Bishop Maurice F. McAuliffe, with Father Cornelius Buckley appointed first pastor. Plans were soon laid for a new church to be raised on the five-acre Wheeler tract at Routes 6 and 172. The new church was dedicated on June 15, 1958, by Archbishop Henry J. O'Brien. In 1986, a liturgical consultant was hired to plan an expansion of parish facilities. Construction got underway, and on Christmas Day 1989, 1200 parishioners first worshiped in their enhanced church. The older church building was later converted into a multi purpose social and educational area.

IMMACULATE CONCEPTION, SOUTHINGTON

Established 1915
Current Pastor: Father David J. Lewandowski
600 households

Though attending Southington's St. Thomas parish, by 1904 the immigrants organized the Guardian Angel

Society in an effort to found a Polish parish. In 1906, a committee of the society asked Bishop Michael A. Tierney for a Polish priest. None was then available. By 1910 Bishop John J. Nilan sent Father John Sullivan to serve the immigrants within St. Thomas Parish. A new Polish Catholic parish was officially approved in September 1915 by Bishop Nilan. Property was secured as a future church site, along with a house to

serve as a rectory. On September 19, 1915, Father Woroniecki celebrated the first parish Mass at a hall belonging to the Polish Falcons. On July 9, 1916, Bishop Nilan dedicated the basement church of Immaculate Conception parish. The completed church was finally dedicated on October 28, 1923.

ST. DOMINIC, SOUTHINGTON

Established 1971
Current Pastor: Father Henry C. Frascadore
2000 households

In June 1970, Archbishop John F. Whealon established a mission within the territory of St. Thomas parish in the northwest section of Southington. Father Walter F. Geraghty was designated pastor. On June 14, the first Mass for the mission was offered at Thalberg School. On February 28, 1971, St. Dominic was established as a parish. Father Geraghty purchased 6.4 scenic acres for a new church near the corner of Flanders Road and Laning Street. On October 14, 1973, Archbishop Whealon dedicated the parish hall, which was then used for Mass until the church proper was completed. On May 31, 1981, Archbishop Whealon dedicated St. Dominic Church, of Spanish-style design in New England brick.

ST. THOMAS, SOUTHINGTON

Established 1860
Current Pastor: Father George F. Lauretti
Parochial Vicar: Father James T. Gregory
2100 households

On Independence Day, 1860 the cornerstone of Saint Thomas Church on Bristol Street in Southington was put in place by Most Reverend Francis P. McFarland, Bishop of Hartford. In December of that year a simple wood frame structure, which could seat 300 people, was dedicated . On September 4, 1862 the Reverend Thomas Drea was appointed the first Pastor as Saint Thomas ceased to be a mission of Saint Rose in Meriden. From the time of its beginning to the present day ten pastors have served Saint Thomas Parish. Milestones in the history of the parish include the establishment of the Saint Thomas Cemetery in the mid 1880's and the building of Saint Thomas School, which opened in 1966. The increasing number of Catholics living in Southington led to the establishment of three new parishes in the

1960's and 70's from the original Saint Thomas Parish. Today the parish of Saint Thomas goes into the 21st century as one of the largest parishes in the Archdiocese, strong and vibrant in the teaching and practicing of the Catholic faith to another generation of Catholics, many of whom are descendents from the original families of the mid 19th century.

SACRED HEART, SUFFIELD

Established 1884
Current Pastor: Father Theodore T. Raczynski
Parochial Vicar: Father Dennis J. Vincenzo
1300 households

The first Mass in Suffield was celebrated in 1876 at the Sheldon Street home of Patrick Devine. Priests from St. Mary in Windsor Locks had begun tending Suffield as their mission by the second half of the 19th century. In 1883 Father Michael Kelly of St. Mary purchased an 11-acre tract as a future Suffield church site. Construction of a wooden edifice began in 1884. Formal dedication occurred on November 30, 1886. In 1913, Sacred Heart was granted parish status, with

Father John E. Clark designated first pastor. In 1984 construction efforts were launched for a modern church. By January of the next year, six classrooms were added to the parish hall to accommodate an ambitious parish agenda. Parishioners were further gladdened as the first Mass in their new colonial-style house of worship was celebrated on July 27, 1985. Contemporary Sacred Heart was dedicated on November 3.

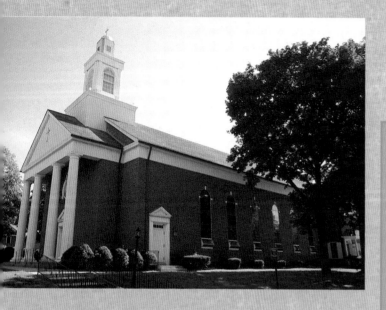

planning, construction of a new church began in 1951. On November 9, 1952, then Bishop Henry J. O'Brien dedicated modern St. Joseph Church, a Georgian style brick edifice.

ST. BERNARD, TARIFFVILLE

Established 1878
Current Pastor: Father Thomas A. Flower
500 households

The first Mass in Tariffville was celebrated in 1846 by Father John Brady. Priests from Hartford, such as Fathers Brady and Peter Walsh, served Tariffville until Father Luke Daly of New Britain assumed this duty in September 1848. In 1850, Father Daly undertook the building of a church on Mountain Road and named it St. Paul's Chapel. On December 10, 1856, the Tariffville chapel became a mission of St. Patrick, Collinsville. In 1876 this church was replaced by a new, larger church and dedicated to St. Bernard on November 23, 1879. This church was located where the present St. Bernard Cemetery now exists. On May 1, 1881, St. Bernard was made a parish with Father John Quinn appointed first pastor. In 1892 the Winthrop Street church mysteriously burned. Land was purchased on Maple Street across from the present-day cemetery, where Bishop Lawrence S. McMahon blessed the cornerstone of a new church on September 25, 1892, later dedicated in 1895.

ST. JOSEPH, SUFFIELD

Polish
Established 1916
Current Pastor: Father William L. Baldyga
200 households

Polish immigrants began settling in the farmlands of Suffield in the 1890s. In 1905, Suffield's Polish immigrants had organized themselves into the St. Joseph Polish Society. In response to the concerns of Apostolic Delegate Archbishop John Bonzano, Bishop John J. Nilan explained that Windsor Locks priests cared for Suffield and that the St. Joseph Society had taken independent action in purchasing land for a church while also intending to find a Polish pastor on their own. About 1915, Father George G. Bartlewski was sent to Sacred Heart Church to minister to Suffield's Polish immigrants. On March 12, 1916, Bishop Nilan finally appointed Father Francis Wladasz as founding pastor of a newly created St. Joseph parish. The new pastor celebrated the first parochial Mass on Easter Sunday 1916 in the Edwin D. Morgan stable purchased earlier by the St. Joseph Society and by now converted into the first parish church. After several years of

McGivney, then in Thomaston, tended the mission. In 1900 Father John Neale was named first resident pastor as the Immaculate Conception mission was made a parish. Father John H. Sheehan purchased another parish cemetery on North Main Street named for St. Mary.

IMMACULATE CONCEPTION, TERRYVILLE

Established 1882
Current Pastor: Father Gerald H. Dziedzic
500 households

At the Eagle Street home of Philip Ryan, Father Michael O'Neil of Waterbury offered the first Mass in Terryville in early 1848. Philip Ryan purchased property on South Main Street in 1858 for a Catholic cemetery named for St. John and donated it for Catholic use. By the mid 19th century, Mass was being offered for all immigrants by visiting priests in private homes or at the Terryville Institute, later used as a public school. Terryville's circuit clerics were from surrounding areas like New Haven, Waterbury, Collinsville, New Britain, Bristol, Watertown and Thomaston. Under Thomaston pastors, a mission church was built in 1882. Immaculate Conception Church opened for Mass on November 5, 1882. On October 14, 1883, Bishop Lawrence S. McMahon dedicated the church. In the late 1880's Knights of Columbus founder Father Michael J.

ST. CASIMIR, TERRYVILLE

Established 1906
Current Pastor: Father Gerald H. Dziedzic
400 households

Polish Immigrants in Terryville increased sharply in number between 1891 and 1900. At first, the immigrants worshiped at Immaculate Conception. Since there was no Polish priest there, however, a movement grew to form a Polish parish. In December 1900, the St. Casimir Society was formed, a Polish fraternal organization that met in the basement of Immaculate Conception. The St. Casimir Society purchased land at 15 Allen Street. By March 1906, Father Joseph Raniszewski was assigned to Terryville with the help of the Apostolic Delegate. This pioneer pastor first offered Mass at Immaculate Conception Church and later in rented halls. Church construction began, and Bishop Tierney dedicated St. Casimir Church on September 1, 1907.

St. Thomas, Thomaston

Established 1869
Current Pastor: Father Harold M. Kearns
Parochial Vicar: Father John E. Cockayne
1500 households

On April 17, 1831, Connecticut's peripatetic pastor, Father James Fitton, preached at the local schoolhouse. Commencing in 1847, Mass was being offered in Plymouth Hollow by visiting Waterbury priests. By 1854, Father Michael O'Neil was celebrating Sunday liturgies monthly at the home of Michael Ryan. Eventually, Academy Hall on Center Green became the place of Sunday Catholic worship. Plymouth Hollow next passed to the care of Bristol in 1864. In March 1871, full parish status was conferred to St. Thomas. On March 31, 1872, St. Thomas basement chapel opened its doors for worship. On October 15 of that year, Bishop Thomas Galberry dedicated the completed parish church. Father Michael J. McGivney, founder of the Knights of Columbus, was appointed second resident pastor on November 30, 1884, and served until his death, on August 14, 1890. The cause for his canonization as a Saint was formally opened in December 1997 by Archbishop Daniel A. Cronin. In 1908, a new St. Thomas Church was dedicated. A new parochial school was dedicated by Archbishop Henry J. O'Brien on October 11, 1964. The school was staffed by the School Sisters of Notre Dame.

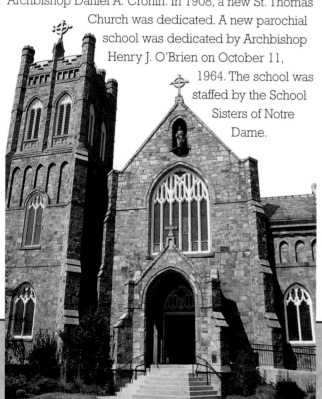

Sacred Heart, Torrington

Slovak
Established 1910
Current Pastor: Father Gerard G. Masters
Parochial Vicar: Father Stephen M. Sledesky
400 households

Slovak men of Torrington gathered themselves into the St. Joseph Society, a chapter of the First Catholic Slovak Union of America. At first, Torrington Slovaks found their spiritual home at St. Francis Church, Torrington. Men of the St. Joseph Society purchased land for a church, aided by the wise counsel of Father Matthew Jankola of SS. Cyril and Methodius Church, Bridgeport. On June 15, 1910, Bishop John J. Nilan appointed Father Gaspar Panik as first pastor of the newly established Sacred Heart. Initially, the recently ordained priest used St. Francis Chapel and later St. Peter Church basement for his congregation. Slovak enthusiasm soon resulted in the dedication of Sacred Heart Church basement by Bishop Nilan on September 3, 1911. On May 30, 1923, Bishop Nilan dedicated the parochial school, which was staffed by the Sisters of SS. Cyril and Methodius. The school closed in 1982.

St. Francis of Assisi, Torrington

Established 1877
Current Pastor: Father Robert W. Ladish
Parochial Vicar: Father John G. Weaver
1300 households

In the 1830's as railroad construction attracted more Irish, Torrington, previously called Wolcottville, became the pastoral responsibility of Hartford. Father James Fitton celebrated the first area Mass in 1835. In November 1842 Torrington fell under Bridgeport's care. The area's six Catholic families then passed to Waterbury's charge from 1847 until 1851. Circuit pastors celebrated Mass in the Academy building on South Main Street where Father Fitton was alleged to have preached earlier. Winsted assumed jurisdiction in 1851. By July 1860, a frame church was erected by Father Michael Mangin. On October 4, 1874, St. Francis of Assisi mission was designated a parish by Bishop Francis P. McFarland, who then named Father Isaias da Scanno, O.F.M., first pastor. Father Patrick Duggan built a new brick Gothic church on a Main Street parcel. St. Francis was both dedicated and consecrated on November 13, 1887. It was allegedly the first parish in the nation claiming this dual ecclesiastical honor. A new school was built in the 1890s staffed by the recently arrived Sisters of Mercy. This original school building was replaced by a modern one in 1961.

*What more could I have done for my vineyard
that I have not done?*

Is. 5:3

St. Mary, Torrington

Polish
Established 1919
Current Pastor: Father Robert W. Ladish
Parochial Vicar: Father John G. Weaver
300 households

During the late 1800's, Polish immigrants were arriving in Torrington, previously known as Wolcottville. About 12 families comprising the Polish enclave at first attended St. Francis Church. In 1901 the immigrants organized a society, incorporated as the Roman Catholic Population of Waterbury. At last, on October 26, 1919, St. Mary parish was created when Father John P. Kowalski was named first pastor. Initially residing at Sacred Heart Church, he celebrated the first Masses for St. Mary in St. Francis chapel. A basement church was completed in 1921 and dedicated on October 5 by Bishop John J. Nilan. The completed church was dedicated on May 30, 1927. On June 12, 1960, ground was broken for a parochial school on the Bryant parcel on Forest Court and dedicated a year later. The school closed in 1984.

St. Peter, Torrington

Italian
Established 1910
Current Pastor: Father Gerard G. Masters
Parochial Vicar: Father Stephen M. Sledesky
2200 households

During the period just after the Civil War, Torrington's Italians were served by Winsted's Father Leo Rizzo da Saracena, O.F.M. Soon the immigrants began attending St. Francis Church. On April 28, 1907, Father Joachim C. Martinez was named pastor of Italian immigrants by Bishop Michael A. Tierney and St. Peter parish was born. On May 11, this prelate presided at the groundbreaking for St. Peter's basement chapel on Center Street. The completed chapel was dedicated on November 15 by Msgr. John Synnott, administrator of the Diocese. Priests from St. Francis attended to St. Peter for a month. When Bishop John J. Nilan announced that St. Peter would be closed, a parish committee successfully appealed for the restoration of a permanent pastor.

In response, on September 25, 1914, Father Salvatore Bonforti was appointed administrator. With the purchase of property on East Main Street in September 1926, the church expansion project progressed. Ground was broken for a new church on March 1, 1927. On May 13, 1928, Bishop Nilan dedicated St. Peter Church. In 1956, Father William P. Botticelli opened a parish school staffed by the Filippini Sisters of New Jersey.

The Polish immigrants who founded St. Hedwig parish, Union City, initially gathered to plan at Alex Sokolowski's hall on August 3, 1902. The Sokolowski committee took another step in October 1904 and acquired the Golden Hill property as a church site. On February 14, 1906, Bishop Tierney dispatched Father Ignacy Maciejewski as the first Polish pastor in Union City. At the first assembly of pastor and people, the parish patron was changed from Our Lady of Czestochowa to St. Hedwig. Father Maciejewski celebrated the first parish Mass at Sokolowski Hall on February 18. By the year's end, a Polish church was built and formally dedicated on June 2, 1907. Father Paul W. Piechocki converted the church hall into a parish school in the 1920s, staffed by the Sisters of the Bernardine Order of St. Francis who had succeeded the Felician Sisters. A new St. Hedwig Church and School complex was dedicated in 1968, staffed by the Daughters of Mary of the Immaculate Conception.

St. Mary, Union City

Established 1907
Current Pastor: Father Richard M. Taberski
500 households

Union City was initially a mission of St. Francis of Assisi Church, Naugatuck. As pastor of the mother parish, Father James O'Reilly Sheridan purchased the Nettleton and Norwood land parcels as a future mission church site. On September 8, 1907, Bishop Michael A. Tierney appointed Father William J. Fanning as first pastor of the new St. Mary parish. Sunday Masses were held in

Sokolowski Hall. In May 1908, ground was broken for a church by contractor John W. Gaffney. Bishop Tierney blessed the cornerstone of the chapel on July 26, 1908. Msgr. John Synott, then President of St. Thomas Seminary, dedicated St. Mary Chapel on December 6. The finished church was dedicated on May 27, 1923.

St. Mary, Unionville

Established 1874
Current Pastor: Father John S. Golas
1100 households

The old church

In 1854, Father Luke Daly of St. Mary in New Britain offered Mass at the home of James Connelly. From 1857 to 1861, Father Patrick O'Dwyer of St. Patrick's in Collinsville assumed responsibility for the fast growing Unionville mission. Father Bernard O'Reilly Sheridan erected a church in 1876 for Unionville Catholics. Unionville was endowed with full canonical status as a parish by Bishop Lawrence S. McMahon. Father Patrick Fox was appointed first resident pastor. Within four months of his arrival, however, Father Fox and his people watched their church burn down on August 16, 1885. In the months ahead, liturgies were temporarily held at the local skating rink. Unionville Catholics broke ground for a new church on the site of the old and soon had the cornerstone blessed on November 29, 1885, by Bishop McMahon. This second church was dedicated on August 22, 1886. It too was damaged by fire in 1891 and once again rebuilt.

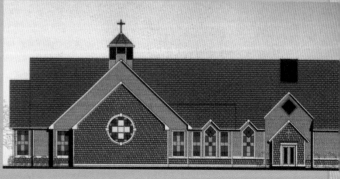

New church under construction.

CHURCH OF THE RESURRECTION, WALLINGFORD

Established 1963
Current Pastor: Monsignor John J. McCarthy
1700 households

Resurrection Parish was established in the fall of 1963 by Archbishop Henry J. O'Brien, who appointed Father George T. O'Neill founding pastor on September 12. Father O'Neill secured Lyman Hall High School for the first parish Masses and resided on Long Hill Road. Land for a church was purchased on Pond Hill Road. The official groundbreaking for the church came on December 19, 1965. Finally, on December 11, the Church of the Resurrection was dedicated by Archbishop O'Brien. In 1969, Resurrection won an award from the National Conference of Religious Architecture for their brick and glass edifice designed by the Russell, Gibson, von Dohlen firm of West Hartford.

MOST HOLY TRINITY, WALLINGFORD

Established 1869
Current Pastor: Father Charles J. MacDonald
Parochial Vicar: Father Dairo Quincha-Diaz
3200 households

On December 22, 1847, a visiting priest from Illinois celebrated the first Wallingford Mass for 12 Catholics at the home of James Hanlon. Wallingford then became the mission of New Haven priest Father Philip O'Reilly until April 1851, when it passed to the care of St. Rose, Meriden. Father Hugh O'Reilly of Meriden bought three lots on North Colony Street as the site of a future church. The Owens home and Union Hall were used as a church and school. On September 1, 1856, Holy Trinity parish was created, with Father Michael A. Wallace appointed first pastor. A barn like church was built, with the cornerstone blessing occurring on November 23, 1857. The parish, however, had reverted to Meriden's mission in August and later in 1861 because of financial shortfalls. Finally, on August 4, 1867, Holy Trinity regained its parish status permanently as Father Hugh Mallon was appointed pastor. After acquiring land from Edward Bristol, Father Mallon built a new church on North Colony Street. Bishop Thomas Galberry blessed the cornerstone on September 24, 1876. On August 9, 1878, a tornado destroyed the old church.

Liturgies were held at the local Baptist Church. The completed church was dedicated by Bishop Lawrence McMahon on November 24, 1887. A school was built and dedicated on September 6, 1914, by Bishop John J. Nilan and staffed by the Sisters of Mercy.

SS. PETER AND PAUL, WALLINGFORD

Established 1924
Current Pastor: Father Daniel J. Karpiey
400 households

By the later part of the 19th century, Polish immigrants in Wallingford were attending Mass at Holy Trinity Church. In the early decades of the 20th century, a Polish Vincentian priest from New Haven's St. Stanislaus Church ministered to the Polish parishioners of Holy Trinity. Bishop John J. Nilan assigned Father Stanislaus Nalewajk as assistant to this Wallingford parish. On September 8, 1924, Father Stanislaus Iciek was designated as temporary administrator of the newly created SS. Peter and Paul parish. Under his direction, the immigrants bought land on North Orchard Street and set about the task of building a church. Until the church was complete, liturgies were celebrated at the Polish National Hall on Prince Street. SS. Peter and Paul Church was opened for the first Mass on May 25, 1925. On June 22, the finished mission-style church was solemnly dedicated by Msgr. Thomas S. Duggan acting on behalf of Bishop Nilan.

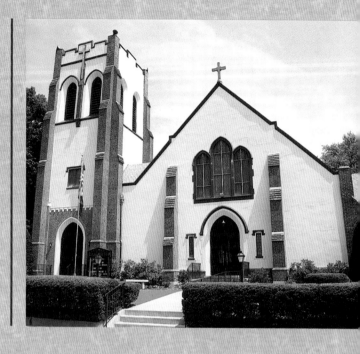

OUR LADY OF PERPETUAL HELP, WASHINGTON DEPOT

Established 1893
Current Pastor: Father Thomas F. Bennett
280 households

Having been the pastoral responsibility of Bridgeport and Norwalk, respectively, before 1851, Washington's few faithful that year passed to Danbury and then to Newtown's jurisdiction in July 1859. By May 1871, St. Francis Xavier parish, New Milford, acquired Washington Depot as a mission. In 1889 construction began on a modest church, and on September 21, 1890, Our Lady of Perpetual Help was dedicated. Father John McGuinness was appointed on April 1, 1908, by Bishop Michael A. Tierney to lead the newly created parish of Our Lady of Perpetual Help. With expansion in mind, Father John F. Callahan purchased 18 acres for a future church site. The new church, of Norman architecture, opened on March 17, 1940. It was later dedicated on April 21 by Bishop Maurice F. McAuliffe.

BLESSED SACRAMENT, WATERBURY

Established 1911
Current Administrator:
Father Michael F.X. Hinkley, S.T.D.
1100 households

Bishop John J. Nilan established Blessed Sacrament parish in the western part of Waterbury on May 7, 1911, appointing Father Terence B. Smith as first pastor. Initially, Mass was offered at nearby St. Patrick Hall on East Main Street. Shortly thereafter, the cornerstone of the new church was blessed by Bishop Nilan in September. The Robbins Street church, on a site selected by Bishop Nilan himself, was dedicated on November 30, 1911. Father John F. Kenney built a parish school on Robinwood Road, dedicated on April 24, 1956, and staffed by the Sisters of the Third Order Regular of St. Francis. The congregation pledged to renovate their church, but with a generous outpouring of support, a new church was built instead and dedicated on January 11, 1981 by Archbishop John F. Whealon. The parish church and school of the Blessed Sacrament continues to be a vibrant community of faith.

IMMACULATE CONCEPTION, WATERBURY

Established 1847
Current Pastor: Father John J. Bevins
Parochial Vicars: Fathers John Curry Gay,
Michael Burke, Maximo Ascencios-Pablo,
M.S.A.; Thomas Simon, M.S.A.;
George White, O.M.I.
1600 households

Initially, the first Waterbury Catholics were the mission responsibility of Hartford's Father James Fitton. Pastoral jurisdiction then passed to the care of New Haven. In 1845, the Catholics rented Washington Hall at the corner of Exchange Place and West Main Street. On November 1, 1847, the mission was created a parish initially under the patronage of St. Peter, with Father Michael O'Neil named first pastor. A vacated Episcopal church was purchased and moved to a location on East Main Street, opening for Mass on Christmas Day 1847. On July 5, 1857, the cornerstone of a new church was blessed and dedicated in December by Bishop Francis P. McFarland. St. Peter's was renamed to honor the recently proclaimed dogma of the Immaculate Conception. In 1863, the pastor converted the old church into a parochial school, staffed by laymen and women. Father John A. Mulcahy built St. Mary School, dedicated on September 4, 1888 by Bishop Lawrence S. McMahon and staffed by the Sisters of Charity. In 1907, Father William J. Slocum organized the initiative to build St. Mary Hospital, the cornerstone of which was blessed on September 22 by Bishop Michael A. Tierney. Father William McGurk chaired the citywide committee of Catholic clergy and laymen to build Waterbury Catholic High School, which opened in 1926. He also undertook the construction of a new church, which was dedicated on May 20, 1928, by Bishop John J. Nilan.

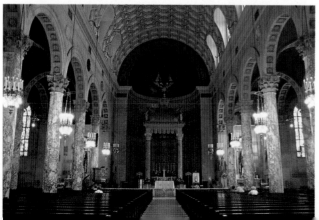

OUR LADY OF FATIMA, WATERBURY

Portuguese
Established 1971
Current Pastor: Father Nelson S. Ribeiro, C.M.
800 households

The Portugese communities of Waterbury and Naugatuck are at the origin of the Parish of Our Lady of Fatima. On May 24, 1959, Vincentian Father Nelson Ribeiro, C.M., first gathered the Portuguese immigrant community for Mass at St. Francis Xavier Church, Waterbury. Portuguese people had also attended Father Ribeiro's liturgies at neighboring St. Francis Church, Naugatuck. The Portuguese congregation at first numbered about 300 families. In 1971, Portuguese spiritual aspirations were crowned when Archbishop John F. Whealon created the parish of Our Lady of Fatima in Waterbury, naming Father Ribeiro as first pastor. As a national parish, Our Lady of Fatima was supported by the Portuguese of both Waterbury and Naugatuck. On Memorial Day 1971, Archbishop Whealon dedicated a new church.

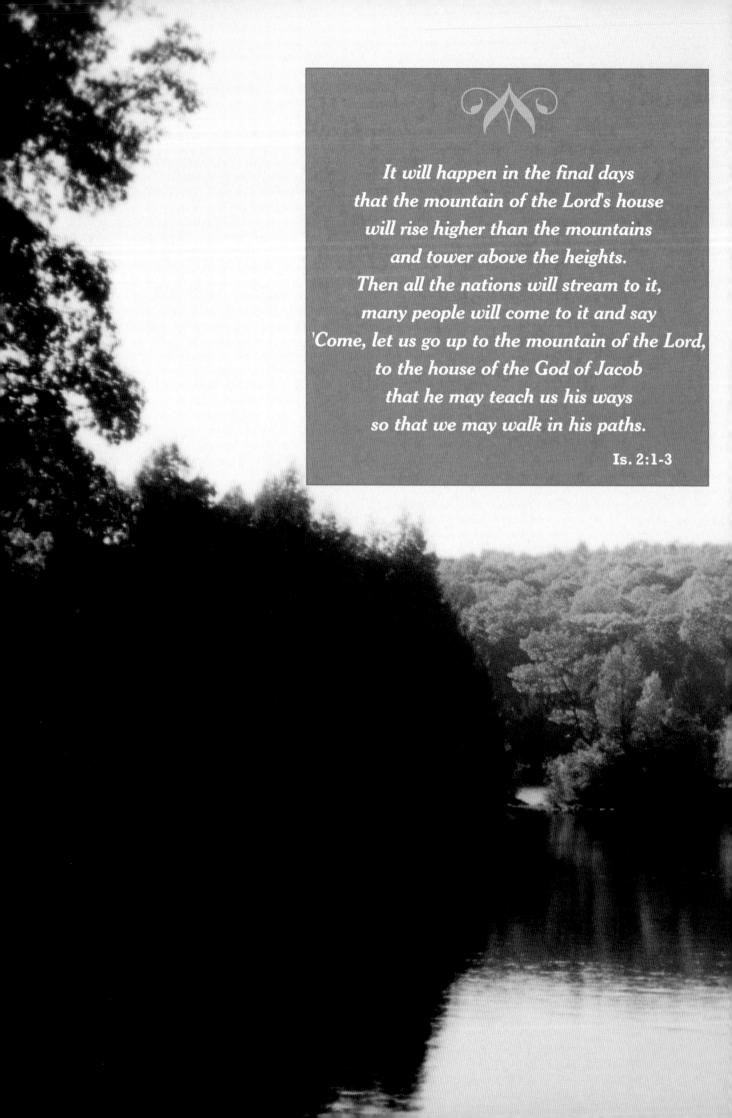

*It will happen in the final days
that the mountain of the Lord's house
will rise higher than the mountains
and tower above the heights.
Then all the nations will stream to it,
many people will come to it and say
'Come, let us go up to the mountain of the Lord,
to the house of the God of Jacob
that he may teach us his ways
so that we may walk in his paths.*

Is. 2:1-3

Our Lady of Loreto, Waterbury

Established 1971
Current Pastor: Monsignor Joseph A. Devine
1000 households

Our Lady of Loreto was established as a mission of Blessed Sacrament parish, Waterbury, in June 1970 by Archbishop John F. Whealon. Father Francis J. Ford was appointed mission pastor. Residing temporarily at Blessed Sacrament, he soon arranged to offer Sunday Mass at the Carrington School. Popularly known as "the mission church of Bunker Hill," Our Lady of Loreto became a parish on June 18, 1971. Plans advanced for a new church, since the former Haddad estate at the corner of Bunker Hill Avenue and Ardsley Road had been purchased in December 1970. Groundbreaking for the church took place in November 1972. The colonial style church of dark brick and concrete was dedicated on December 23, 1973, by Archbishop Whealon.

Our Lady of Lourdes, Waterbury

Italian
Established 1899
Current Pastor: Father Ronald A. Ferraro
800 households

In the spring of 1888, famed Franciscan Padre Leo Rizzo da Saracena, O.F.M., offered Mass for the Italian immigrants of Waterbury at Immaculate Conception Church. Beginning in 1894, Father Farrell Martin of St. Cecilia parish attended the Italian population for five years. Born in Palestine, Father Michael Karam was appointed founding pastor of Our Lady of Lourdes. On June 11, he offered the premier parish Mass at a renovated barn loft on Canal Street. New worshiping quarters and a rectory on South Main Street were acquired by the end of the month. Bishop Tierney dedicated the new chapel on November 19, 1899. It soon became apparent, however, that a larger church was needed. A basement chapel opened for Mass in July 1904. The finished church, modeled after the Roman church of Santa Francesca Romana, was dedicated on February 14, 1909, by Monsignor John Synnott.

Our Lady of Mt. Carmel, Waterbury

Italian
Established 1923
Current Pastor: Father James H. Smith
1800 households

Italian immigrants to Waterbury's Brooklyn Town Plot neighborhood originally attended Our Lady of Lourdes Church. On June 26, 1923, Bishop John J. Nilan appointed Father Michael J. Lynch first pastor of a new parish named at first for St. Philip Neri. Father Lynch became responsible for the spiritual needs of about 4500 people, for whom he offered Mass in the basement of St. Patrick Church until April 1924. Father Lynch was busy supervising the construction of a basement church on

land secured at the corner of Highland Avenue and America Street. On April 13, 1924, Bishop Nilan dedicated the basement chapel, renaming the parish at this time for Our Lady of Mount Carmel. In 1939, plans were set in motion for constructing the church superstructure in the Lombard Romanesque style. On July 14, 1940, then Bishop Henry J. O'Brien officiated at cornerstone ceremonies. The formal dedication took place on December 8. On September 8, 1957, the parish plant was rounded out with the dedication of a new Congress Avenue school and convent by Archbishop O'Brien. The school was staffed by the Daughters of Wisdom from Litchfield.

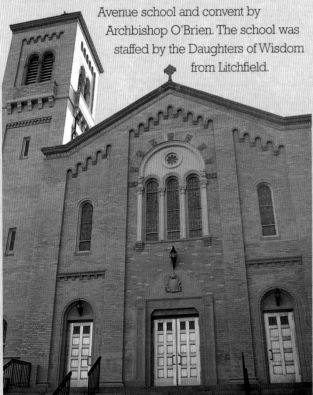

Sacred Heart, Waterbury

Established 1885
Current Administrator: Father Kevin G. Donovan
200 households

Bishop Lawrence S. McMahon authorized Father William A. Harty of Immaculate Conception Church, Waterbury, to announce the establishment of Sacred Heart parish on February 15, 1885. First pastor Father Hugh Treanor offered Sacred Heart's initial Masses in St. Patrick Chapel at East Main Street and Phoenix Avenue. Father Treanor acquired the Porter estate and hired noted New York architect Patrick C. Keely to design the parish church. The church cornerstone was blessed on August 16, 1885. A basement chapel was dedicated by Bishop McMahon on March 14, 1886. On November 28, 1889, Bishop McMahon dedicated Sacred Heart. Father Thomas Shelley built an elementary school, dedicated on August 6, 1906 and staffed by the Sisters of Mercy. Father John J. Fitzgerald organized Sacred Heart Academy for girls in 1922, the first parish high school in the Diocese. In 1927, the parish organized the city's first Catholic Boy Scout troop. The Academy became coeducational in 1938. In 1975, Sacred Heart High school ceased to be a parish institution and joined the network of archdiocesan high schools.

ST. ANNE, WATERBURY

French
Established 1886
Current Administrator: Father Alvin J. LeBlanc
400 households

The French-Canadian community of Waterbury first met on Grand Street at a former Universalist Chapel in 1886. Appeals were made to Bishop Lawrence S. McMahon, who on April 15, 1886, named Fr. Joseph Fones of Watertown as the founding pastor of a new parish under the patronage of St. Anne. Property was subsequently purchased on South Main Street and on September 2, 1888, Bishop McMahon blessed the cornerstone of a new parish church which was dedicated on January 27, 1889. The original parish school opened in 1890, initially staffed by the Sisters of the Congregation of Notre Dame and subsequently, for the better part of a century, by the Daughters of the Holy Spirit. A new school was built in the mid-1950's. However, after 102

years of service, the parish school closed its doors in 1992. The present majestic Gothic church was begun in 1906 and a basement chapel was dedicated on Christmas Day, 1908. Completed in granite, the new parish church was dedicated by Bishop John J. Nilan on December 17, 1922 to the great rejoicing of the congregation. In the decades which followed, thousands of French-Canadian families were ministered to from this great church edifice which still shines forth as a beacon of faith and tradition to its faithful and to all passers-by.

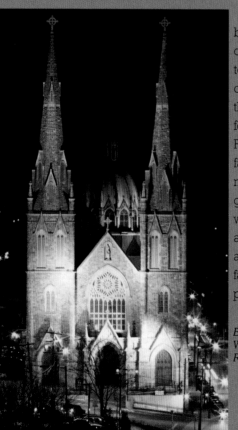

By permission of Waterbury Republican-American

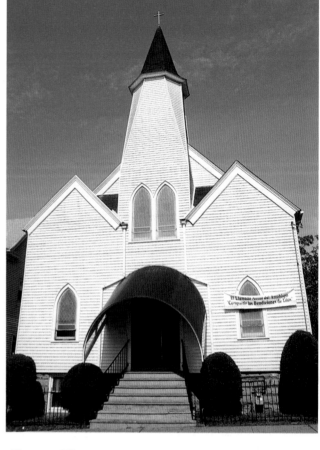

ST. CECILIA, WATERBURY

German
Established 1893
Current Pastor: Father Kevin J. Gray
1000 households

On April 24, 1892, a core group of Waterbury German Catholics covenanted themselves into the Holy Family Society, intending to found their own parish. On October 9, 1892, Father Farrell Martin gathered German Catholics in St. Patrick Hall. On November 18, Bishop Lawrence S. McMahon appointed Father Martin pastor of St. Cecilia parish. The first parish Mass was offered on November 20, 1892, at the hall of Notre Dame Academy. The cornerstone of a new Gothic church was blessed on July 29, 1894, by Bishop Michael A. Tierney. On November 18, 1894, the completed church edifice was dedicated. September 1907 brought the opening of a social hall and a short-lived parish school on Jefferson Street. Urban redevelopment in the 1960s soon resulted in a relocation of the parish church from Scovill Street to a former Advent Christian church building that had been purchased. Handsomely refurbished, the Cherry Street St. Cecilia Church was dedicated by Auxiliary Bishop Joseph F. Donnelly in 1966.

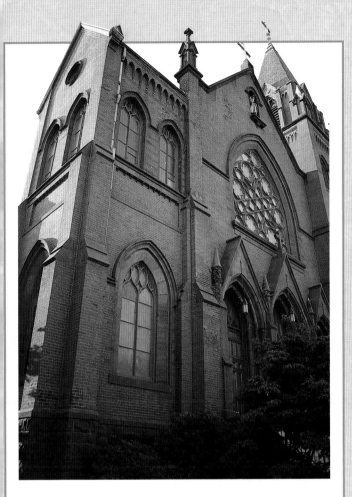

ST. FRANCIS XAVIER, WATERBURY

Established 1896
Current Pastor: Father Paul J. Pace
1000 households

About 500 families in Waterbury's south end were attending either St. Patrick or Immaculate Conception parish as the nineteenth century was nearing an end. Bishop Michael A. Tierney recognized their need for autonomy by appointing Father Jeremiah J. Curtin first pastor of a new city parish on December 3, 1895. Originally St. Joseph, the new parish's name was soon changed to St. Francis Xavier to avoid confusion with another area parish. Initially, Father Curtin celebrated parish liturgies in a South Main Street auditorium. The arrangement lasted until a frame church was erected and opened for Mass on April 22, 1896. The first Church of St. Francis Xavier was dedicated on May 30, 1896. Groundbreaking for a new center of parish worship occurred on April 17, 1902. Bishop Thomas B. Beavan of Springfield dedicated the new church of St. Francis Xavier on March 24, 1907. Dedicated on February 10, 1924, was another faith-generated institution, a parish school located on Baldwin Street and staffed by the Sisters of St. Joseph of Chambery.

ST. JOSEPH, WATERBURY

Lithuanian
Established 1894
Current Administrator: Father John L. Williams
300 households

Lithuanian immigrants in Waterbury usually attended Mass at St. Patrick Church, but they were also visited by two Brooklyn, New York, priests, Fathers Antanas Varnagiris and Matthew Juodysius. On March 28, 1894, Bishop Michael A. Tierney appointed Father Joseph Zebris as pastor of the new St. Joseph parish in response to local Lithuanian petitions on his behalf. Father Zebris offered Mass for his new congregation on April 1, 1894, in the Mitchell block on Bank Street. On December 25, the pastor blessed a new frame church at the corner of Congress and John Streets. In 1904 a new brick church was built and dedicated in 1905 on the site of the original one. On January 6, 1906, three refugee French Daughters of the Holy Ghost joined the parish,  learned Lithuanian, and soon staffed the burgeoning parish school, which operated in the former church building that had been moved to John Street. An additional school building was constructed in 1912-13. Father Joseph J. Valantiejus founded an orphanage to care for victims of the 1918 influenza epidemic and built a new school in 1925. St. Joseph holds the distinction of being the first Lithuanian worshiping community in Connecticut.

St. Leo the Great, Waterbury

Established 1974
Current Pastor: Father Joseph F. Gorman
800 households

On July 1, 1971, Father A. Leo Spodnik was assigned by Archbishop John F. Whealon to organize a mission in Waterbury's east end within the territory of SS. Peter and Paul Church. Temporarily residing at the rectory of the mother church, the mission pastor had charge of about 250 families, for whom he celebrated the first mission Mass at the East Farms School gym on July 25, 1971. In early 1972, the congregation voted to adopt St. Leo the Great as their patron. About 3.5 acres of land, centrally located on Bentwood Drive, were purchased in March as the site for a church. Beginning early in 1973, liturgies were offered in Rotella School. In May 1974, St. Leo had achieved full parish status, with Father Spodnik as first pastor. Groundbreaking for a new church was held on June 25. Archbishop Whealon dedicated the church on December 12, 1976. In June of 1991, second pastor Father Joseph F. Gorman was appointed by Archbishop John F. Whealon.

St. Lucy, Waterbury

Italian
Established 1926
Current Pastor: Father Ronald A. Ferraro
500 households

St. Lucy parish was established on October 9, 1926, for Italian immigrants in the north end of Waterbury. Bishop John J. Nilan appointed Father Felix Scoglio as first pastor of the city's third Italian national parish. North end Italians had attended Our Lady of Lourdes Church before Bishop Nilan dedicated their own church on Branch Street on May 8, 1927. Before the structure was erected, the St. Lucy congregation worshiped at the Y.M.C.A. On November 28, 1954, another parochial milestone was reached as St. Lucy School was dedicated on Griggs Street. Initially staffed by lay teachers, the school became the responsibility of the Felician Sisters from Enfield in 1957. With great pride, Father Scoglio broke ground for a new church on June 24, 1962. Dedicated by Archbishop Henry J. O'Brien on June 27, 1964, the new St. Lucy Church was a stunning replica of Santa Francesca Church in Rome. In 1977, the Felician Sisters left the parish school and were replaced by the Melkite Sisters.

ST. MARGARET, WATERBURY

Established 1910
Current Pastor: Father Joseph E. Looney
900 households

Taken from the territory of Waterbury's Immaculate Conception parish in the northwestern part of the city, St. Margaret was the first new parish of Bishop John J. Nilan's episcopate. On July 29, 1910, he appointed as founding pastor Father Edward J. Brennan, who had just returned from duty as the Diocese's first Navy chaplain. On July 31, Father Brennan celebrated the first parish Mass at Immaculate Conception's St. Patrick Hall on East Main Street. Bishop Nilan had earlier bought five acres at Willow and Ludlow Streets as the future site of St. Margaret's parish plant. Bishop Nilan dedicated St. Margaret's temporary church on October 16, 1910. Soon, St. Margaret School was established in 1915. At last, construction began on the permanent church in 1955. On June 9, 1957, Auxiliary Bishop John F. Hackett dedicated the church of modified Gothic design.

ST. MICHAEL, WATERBURY

Established 1897
Current Pastor: Father Ronald Gliatta, O.F.M.
1000 households

Catholics of the Waterville section of Waterbury were first served from Immaculate Conception. On December 2, 1895, they passed to the care of St. Patrick Church. Father Joseph M. Gleeson then purchased land for a mission church on Thomaston Street from James Coughlin and Patrick Thompson. Sunday Mass was offered in Ford's Hall until the church was ready. On August 8, 1897, Bishop Michael A. Tierney dedicated the mission church to St. Michael the Archangel. On March 25, 1902, prodigious growth led to the conferring of parish status as Bishop Tierney named Father Matthew J. Traynor first pastor of St. Michael. Auxiliary Bishop John F. Hackett dedicated the new parish church and rectory on St. Michael Drive on August 21, 1966. St. Thomas Church, Waterbury, established in 1898, merged with St. Michael's in 1997.

St. Patrick, Waterbury

Established 1880
Current Pastor: Father John L. Williams
400 households

On February 1, 1880, Bishop Lawrence S. McMahon asked Father John H. Duggan of Colchester to organize St. Patrick parish in the southwest part of Waterbury. On February 19, the priest purchased acreage upon which a future parish plant could be built. In April Father Duggan was officially named pastor of the new parish. On May 23, Father Duggan offered the first parish Mass at St. Patrick Chapel, a former Methodist chapel on East Main Street at the corner of Phoenix Avenue. Owned by Immaculate Conception, the building would host St. Patrick liturgies until the new basement chapel was completed. The cornerstone of the future church was blessed on October 16, 1881. The chapel was later dedicated and opened for worship on December 17, 1882. Father Joseph M. Gleeson started a parish school in 1900 at a former public school building that had been purchased by his predecessor, relocated to Porter Street, and refitted as a lyceum. The Sisters of St. Joseph of Chambery staffed the parochial institution. Father Gleeson completed the granite superstructure of St. Patrick Church, which was dedicated on January 18, 1903 by Bishop Tierney with Cardinal Gibbons of Baltimore and other prelates in attendance. Because of structural problems with the lyceum building, St. Patrick School was closed in 1910.

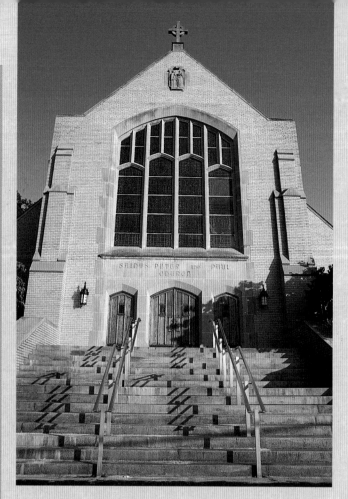

SS. Peter and Paul, Waterbury

Established 1920
Current Pastor: Monsignor James G. Coleman
Parochial Vicar: Father Joseph R. Cronin
2500 households

SS. Peter and Paul parish was established on April 15, 1920, by Bishop John J. Nilan to serve the Catholic population in Waterbury's east end. Named founding pastor was Father Thomas P. Mulcahy, who used the basement of Sacred Heart Church for parish Mass. Acreage had been acquired by the Diocese in 1916 in anticipation of parochial needs. Events moved forward nicely as groundbreaking for a church took place on June 29, 1920. The church cornerstone was blessed by Auxiliary Bishop John G. Murray on November 28. The dedication of the basement church came on April 3, 1921. Zeal for parochial education produced an eight-room school, dedicated on November 21, 1926, and staffed by the Sisters of Mercy. The complete church superstructure was dedicated by Archbishop Henry J. O'Brien on September 11, 1955.

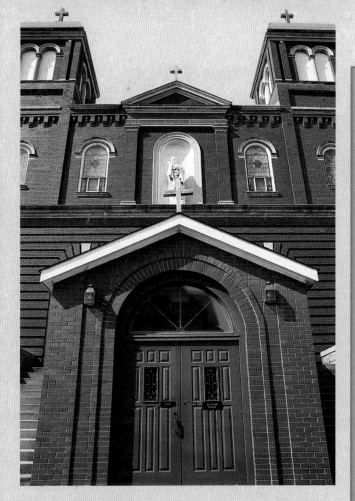

St. Stanislaus Kostka, Waterbury

Polish
Established 1913
Current Pastor: Father Stephen H. Bzdyra
200 households

On February 14, 1909, at a Hobart Street meeting, Joseph Wojdyla assumed a leadership role in gathering his countrymen into the St. Stanislaus Kostka Society. Another key decision then taken was that all Poles would attend St. Cecilia Church. On July 7, 1912, Bishop John J. Nilan appointed Father Ignatius Maciejewski as administrator of a Polish parish in Waterbury. The priest soon celebrated the first parish Mass in the chapel of Our Lady of Lourdes Church, which the immigrants had rented. St. Stanislaus parish became legally incorporated on January 30, 1913. Land on East Farm Street was purchased from the Immaculate Conception parish for a church. On August 13, 1914, Bishop Nilan named Father Theodore Zimmerman first resident pastor. The gray granite foundation having been laid, the church cornerstone was blessed on September 14, 1914. The first Mass was celebrated in the completed edifice on October 24, 1915. The completed church superstructure was dedicated on September 26, 1926.

St. John the Evangelist, Watertown

Established 1878
Current Pastor: Father John M. Cooney
Parochial Vicar: Father J. Daniel McElheron
1800 households

Waterbury's Father Michael O'Neil offered the first Watertown liturgy in 1855 at the Cutler Street residence of John McGowan. Waterbury priests continued to offer monthly Mass at Citizen's Hall, a former Episcopal church, until 1866, when Watertown passed to Bristol's jurisdiction. After reverting to Waterbury's charge from 1868 to 1871, Watertown then passed to Thomaston's care. Father Eugene Gaffney of Thomaston acquired land at the corner of Main and Woodruff Streets as a proposed church site. In November 1877, Bishop Thomas Galberry blessed the St. John cornerstone. The mission church was dedicated on March 24, 1878. St. John was created a parish in November 1884, when Father Joseph Fones was named first pastor. During his tenure in Watertown, Father James H. O'Donnell wrote his History of the Diocese of Hartford in 1900. St. John's became the smallest diocesan parish to found a school, which opened in 1908. Four years later, the School Sisters of Notre Dame assumed teaching duties. On April 11, 1959, a new colonial style church on Main Street and Academy Hill was at last dedicated by Archbishop Henry J. O'Brien.

St. Brigid, West Hartford

Established 1919
Current Pastor: Father Francis T. Carter
1200 households

St. Brigid had the distinction of being the first Catholic parish in West Hartford. Most Catholics residing there had been attending St. Lawrence O'Toole, pastors of which were assigned the chief responsibility for the Elmwood section of West Hartford. The first Mass in the

section was celebrated by Father Peter J. Dolin on Christmas Day 1916 at the New Departure Company. During the preceding August, however, land had been purchased for the construction of a mission chapel. On September 16, 1917, Bishop John J. Nilan dedicated a wooden chapel that was placed under the patronage of St. Brigid. The mission was made a parish on August 4, 1919, with Father William F. Odell as first pastor. His successor, Father William Brewer, demolished the old frame chapel and built a new brick church on the same New Britain Avenue site, dedicated by Archbishop O'Brien on April 29, 1951. Construction began on an 18-room school and convent. St. Brigid School opened in September 1960, staffed by the Sisters of the Cross and Passion. They were eventually succeeded by the Sisters of Mercy and then the Congregation of Notre Dame.

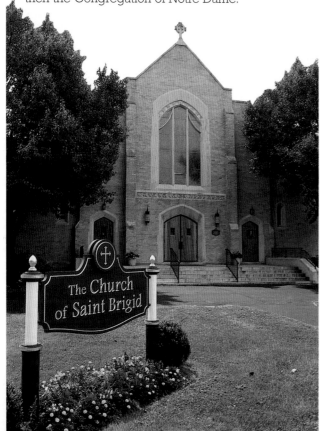

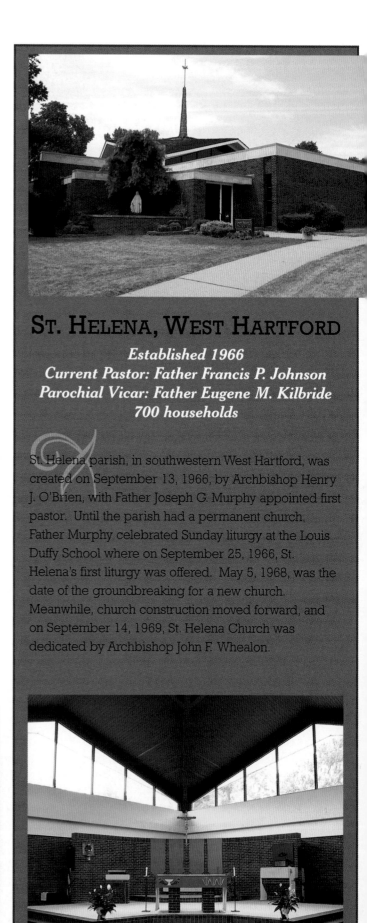

St. Helena, West Hartford

Established 1966
Current Pastor: Father Francis P. Johnson
Parochial Vicar: Father Eugene M. Kilbride
700 households

St. Helena parish, in southwestern West Hartford, was created on September 13, 1966, by Archbishop Henry J. O'Brien, with Father Joseph G. Murphy appointed first pastor. Until the parish had a permanent church, Father Murphy celebrated Sunday liturgy at the Louis Duffy School where on September 25, 1966, St. Helena's first liturgy was offered. May 5, 1968, was the date of the groundbreaking for a new church. Meanwhile, church construction moved forward, and on September 14, 1969, St. Helena Church was dedicated by Archbishop John F. Whealon.

St. Mark the Evangelist, West Hartford

Established 1942
Current Pastor: Father Thomas J. Sas
900 households

Because building materials were scarce during World War II, only a portable church was possible at the time of the parish's founding. The original St. Mark Church, located on South Quaker Lane, was a narrow building with a heating grate running through its center. A fire of suspicious origin destroyed it on June 24, 1944. The worship space was relocated to the hall of St. Thomas the Apostle parish until a new church was built. Bishop Henry J. O'Brien dedicated a new St. Mark on the site of the first church on September 30, 1945. St. Mark's Parish Center was dedicated in 1971 by Archbishop John F. Whealon, with ample space for classrooms and an assembly hall.

St. Peter Claver, West Hartford

Established 1966
Current Pastor: Father Joseph P. McGarry
1200 households

On September 9, 1966, Archbishop Henry J. O'Brien created St. Peter Claver parish, West Hartford, from territory of St. Thomas the Apostle. For the founding pastor the Archbishop chose a veteran priest and dean of Catholic secondary education in the Archdiocese, Father John T. Shugrue. Masses were held at the Braeburn School until a church could be built, with the first Mass held in October 1966. In the summer of 1968 groundbreaking took place. By the fall of 1969, a spacious parish center was complete.

Church construction was advanced enough to allow for the celebration of Christmas midnight Mass in 1969. Hopes were marvelously fulfilled on May 3, 1970, with the formal dedication of the new church. For three consecutive years after its completion, it won first prize for church architecture in Connecticut, New England, and the nation.

St. Thomas the Apostle, West Hartford

Established 1921
Current Pastor: Father Arthur J. Murphy
Parochial Vicars: Fathers Edward M. Moran, Patrick J. Curran
1400 households

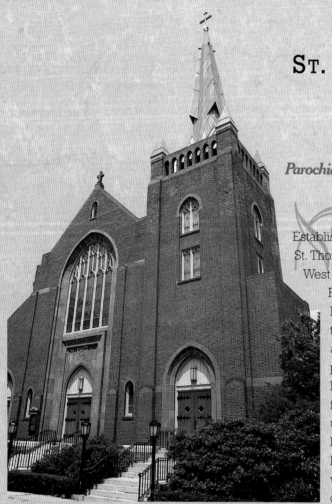

Established in early November 1920 by Bishop John J. Nilan, St. Thomas the Apostle became the second Catholic parish in West Hartford. Founding pastor Father John F. Callahan offered the first parochial Mass in a portable wooden edifice at the southwest corner of Quaker Lane and Boulevard. In 1923, Father Callahan purchased land at the corner of Dover Road and Farmington Avenue as a site for the parish church. Construction got underway, and on November 7, 1926, a basement chapel was dedicated by Bishop Nilan. The parish's next project was construction of a school. On April 28, 1937, the cornerstone of St. Thomas the Apostle School was blessed. Located on Dover Road and staffed by the Sisters of Mercy, it was dedicated on September 12. In 1948, the Ursuline Sisters succeeded the Sisters of Mercy. Bishop Henry J. O'Brien solemnly dedicated the upper church on September 16, 1951. In 1989, St. Thomas youngsters began attending St. Timothy Middle School, a joint educational venture with St. Timothy parish.

St. Timothy, West Hartford

Established 1958
Current Pastor: Father Henry P. Cody
1000 households

Archbishop Henry J. O'Brien established West Hartford's St. Timothy parish on August 7, 1958, and named Father Francis S. O'Neill as pastor. On September 14, 1958, the first parish Mass was held in the auditorium of King Philip School. The Archdiocese had acquired a North Main Street site for the new parish on November 7, 1957. A brick and cinder block chapel holding 75 people was blessed on December 4, 1958. Archbishop O'Brien presided at the dedication of St. Timothy Church and School on June 19, 1960. The school was staffed by the Dominican Sisters of St. Mary of the Springs. A new parish center was dedicated on December 12, 1971, by Archbishop John F. Whealon. In September 1989, St. Timothy Middle School was created, a joint educational venture with St. Thomas the Apostle parish.

Our Lady of Victory, West Haven

Established 1935
Current Pastor: Father Mark S. Suslenko
Parochial Vicar: Father Ronald J. Osborne
2600 households

In 1935, Bishop Maurice F. McAuliffe appointed Father John W. Walsh pastor for the Prospect Beach section of West Haven. Under the patronage of Our Lady of Victory, the new parish began its services at the Colonial Inn, a rambling resort on Long Island Sound, bought by Father Walsh for use as a church. The church was gutted by a fire that required the relocation of Masses to the West Shore Fire House while the church was being repaired. Father Thomas McMahon purchased 10 acres of land on Jones Hill Road for a church site and then commenced an ambitious fund drive. Groundbreaking for a new church was held on July 24, 1955. On October 28, 1956, Archbishop Henry J. O'Brien dedicated the modern Our Lady of Victory parish plant. Parish facilities were completed during the early 1960's with the building of a parochial school.

St. John Vianney, West Haven

Established 1965
Current Pastor: Father Mark S. Suslenko
Parochial Vicar: Father Ronald J. Osborne
1000 households

In 1909, Father Jeremiah Curtin, pastor at St. Lawrence Church, West Haven, encouraged the founding of a mission in the West Shore community of Savin Rock. A frame chapel was raised at the corner of Kelsey Avenue and Captain Thomas Boulevard. Bishop John J. Nilan dedicated the chapel on June 5, 1910. For 31 years, Mass was celebrated at this mission only during the summer. The chapel had been thoroughly remodeled for year round use when the Catholic population began to swell by the World War II era. On May 24, 1941, Bishop Maurice F. McAuliffe blessed a new cornerstone and dedicated the mission to St. John Vianney. Post war growth prompted Archbishop Henry J. O'Brien to make the mission a full parish in 1965 with the naming of Father Joseph W. Reynolds as resident pastor. Father Reynolds embarked upon building a parish complex that would include church, hall, and rectory. The interconnected parish plant, located on Captain Thomas Boulevard, was dedicated on November 7, 1971, by Archbishop John F. Whealon.

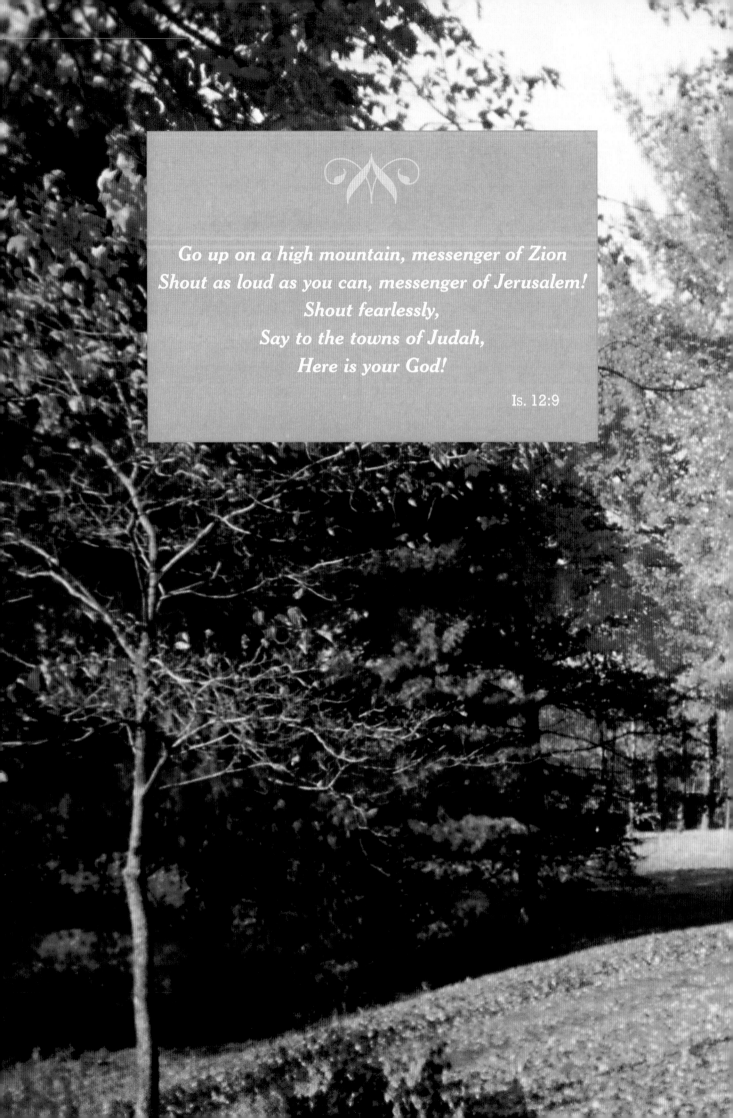

Go up on a high mountain, messenger of Zion
Shout as loud as you can, messenger of Jerusalem!
Shout fearlessly,
Say to the towns of Judah,
Here is your God!

Is. 12:9

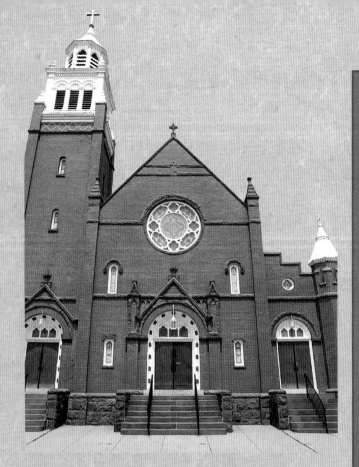

French Canadians of New Haven were numerous enough to warrant their own parish by the late 19th century. On May 18, 1889, Bishop Lawrence S. McMahon named Father Francis J. E. Bourret founding pastor of St. Louis. A week later, he celebrated the first parish Mass in the hall of St. Patrick School. In early June, the place of worship was moved to Loomis Hall and by December to the Knights of Columbus Hall. A dwelling at 515 Chapel Street was purchased, and the first floor was renovated as a chapel. Bishop McMahon dedicated the chapel in July 1890. A school for about 25 pupils was first convened in the church basement in November 1893. Father Joseph A. N. Grenier undertook construction of a new church at the corner of Chestnut and Chapel Streets that was dedicated on August 5, 1906, by Bishop Michael A. Tierney. In September a new school opened in the former church and by 1925, the school was operating out of its own building. After a tragic fire of August 29, 1960, destroyed the church, Mass was celebrated for two years in the school basement. A dramatic decision was then made in 1962 to relocate the entire parish plant to 10 acres on Saw Mill Road and Bull Hill Lane in West Haven. Previously an ethnic parish, St. Louis now became territorial as well. Groundbreaking for the new parish plant including church, rectory, convent, and school was held in July 1964. On September 12, St. Louis' new parish plant was dedicated by Archbishop Henry J. O'Brien. St. Louis School closed in 1989.

ST. LAWRENCE, WEST HAVEN

Established 1886
Current Pastor: Father Mark R. Jette
950 households

Long before it officially became West Haven, Catholics of the section of what was then Orange were pastorally served by a variety of jurisdictions, including New Haven and Milford. In April 1886, West Haven's Catholics advanced as a worshiping community as Bishop Lawrence S. McMahon blessed the cornerstone of their wooden church, dedicated on August 19, 1888. St. Lawrence then reverted to Sacred Heart, New Haven, as its mission in 1892. Three years later, Father Jeremiah J. Curtin was designated resident pastor and St. Lawrence acquired parish status. Initially an enclave of 200, the congregation quickly required a large church. The cornerstone was blessed on June 21, 1903, and the completed church was dedicated

shortly thereafter. The parish erected a summer chapel for the busy Old Savin Rock recreational area in 1910. The pastor added to the plant with a school dedicated in 1917 and staffed by the Sisters of St. Joseph of Chambery.

ST. PAUL, WEST HAVEN

Established 1916
Current Administrator: Father Salvatore J. Rosa
1000 households

A prolific growth among Catholics of West Haven's north end occasioned the creation of St. Paul parish. Bishop John J. Nilan appointed Father Francis M. Murray as founding pastor on September 2, 1916.

Father Murray first offered Sunday Mass at Harugari Hall on Campbell Avenue. The hall was the site of parish Masses until June 10, 1917, when Bishop Nilan dedicated a basement chapel located at First Avenue and Alling Street. Father Michael P. Barry built a chapel of ease on Dalton Street, dedicated on June 9, 1937. A larger church, to be erected on the foundation of the basement church, was constructed and dedicated on October 9, 1955 by Archbishop O'Brien.

ST. CATHERINE OF SIENA, WEST SIMSBURY

Established 1971
Current Pastor: Father Richard R. Russell
800 households

In June 1970, Archbishop John F. Whealon created St. Catherine of Siena as a mission of St. Mary, Simsbury, and appointed Father John D. Hurley as pastor. Masses were offered in private homes and the Tootin Hills School until 1971. Masses were then celebrated in the spacious new rectory parlor on Stratton Brook Road. In 1971, St. Catherine of Siena reached parish status. In December 1974, Archbishop Whealon dedicated St. Catherine of Siena Church and hall.

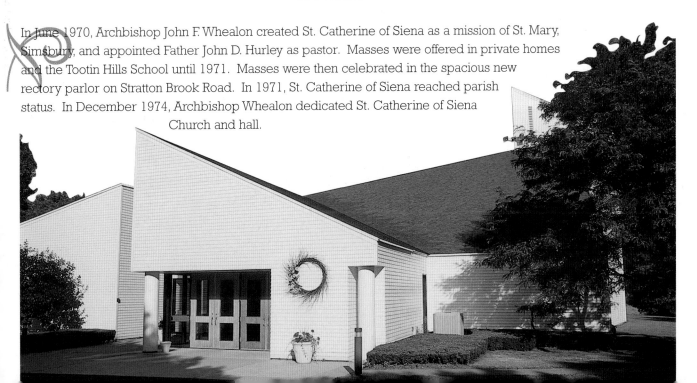

CORPUS CHRISTI, WETHERSFIELD

Established 1941
Co-Pastors: Fathers Thomas B. Campion and David W. Lonergan
2500 Households

Increases in the Catholic population of Wethersfield precipitated the building of a new church. Originally believed to replace the fire-damaged Sacred Heart Church, the new building on the Silas Deane Highway was dedicated as Corpus Christi Church on November 26, 1938. It was officially established as the second Catholic parish in Wethersfield on September 27, 1941 with Father Francis E. Nash appointed first pastor. In 1958, a group of parishioners approached Father Nash about establishing a parish school. Funding was quickly organized by canvassing the entire parish. Land was purchased from the Town of Wethersfield and construction began in 1959. By the end of 1960, the 16-room building was completed. Archbishop Henry J. O'Brien dedicated the school, auditorium and convent on June 4, 1961. The religious community of Sisters of the Cross and Passion staffed the school from 1960 until 1973. Since that time, members of the laity have staffed the school. From the mid-70s until 1996, groups overseen by the archdiocese's Catholic Family Services utilized the convent building. By the early 1990s, the school experienced a growth in requests for admission. School expansion moved the Pre-K program into the convent building by the fall of 1997. In 1999, work began to add six classrooms to the south side of the school. This undertaking was made possible by the generous bequest of a Corpus Christi parishioner as well as the generosity of parishioners and school alumni who supported the building program. In 1968, Father Robert W. Shanley was named Corpus Christi's second pastor. He admired architectural simplicity, utilizing a colonial motif of plain blue and white décor to oversee changes in the church interior to conform to liturgical guidelines of the Second Vatican Council. When new pastors came to Corpus Christi in 1983, the old wooden Stations of the Cross were taken out of storage and painted to compliment this simple yet welcoming décor. Corpus Christi celebrated 60 years of parish life with a Mass of Thanksgiving and an anniversary reception on September 23, 2001.

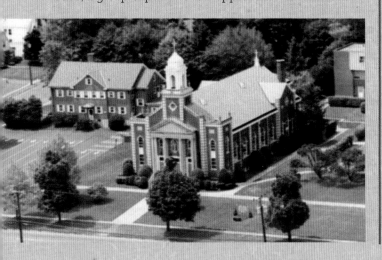

INCARNATION, WETHERSFIELD

Established 1963
Current Pastor: Father John F. Edwards
Parochial Vicar: Father James M. Moran
2100 households

On September 12, 1963, Incarnation parish, Wethersfield, was established and named by Archbishop Henry J. O'Brien.

Father John J. Crawford was appointed first pastor. The first parish Mass was celebrated on September 15 at the Samuel Webb Junior High School. A fund drive for a church began in April 1964. By fall, ground was broken and church construction went forward. Archbishop O'Brien dedicated the Church of the Incarnation on January 23, 1966.

Sacred Heart, Wethersfield

Established 1876
Co-Pastors: Fathers Thomas B. Campion and David W. Lonergan
450 households

Sacred Heart of Jesus was the first Catholic parish in historic Wethersfield. Tradition has it that the first Mass in Revloutionary Connecticut was offered in Wethersfield for the army of French General Rochambeau. In 1877, the Wethersfield congregation became a mission of St. Mary in East Hartford. This first Catholic church in Wethersfield was erected on Garden Street, on a lot purchased in 1876. The building was dedicated on May 29, 1881 as a mission of St. Lawrence O'Toole in Hartford. On September 1, 1897, Bishop Michael A. Tierney made Sacred Heart a parish. In 1923, parish growth was acknowledged with the purchase of the Meggat Seed Warehouse and adjacent family home situated on Hartford Avenue, which was then remodeled into a spacious church with a social hall. This second Sacred Heart Church was blessed on Easter Sunday in 1924. In early 1938, a disastrous fire struck Sacred Heart, causing extensive damage. The congregation was forced to reoccupy the original Garden Street church. After the fire, there were plans for a new church to be constructed on the Silas Deane Highway. However, when construction was completed in 1939, the new building was dedicated as Corpus Christi Church. Consequently, the fire-damaged church was renovated and reconverted into the Sacred Heart sanctuary, then blessed on April 4, 1943. In the 1950s, permission to repair both the inside and outside of the church was

denied due to the poor condition of the building. Instead, it was recommended that the parish request permission to build a new church. Groundbreaking took place in September of 1962 and on June 29, 1963 Archbishop Henry J. O'Brien dedicated the new - third - Sacred Heart Church. On September 1, 1995, Sacred Heart Church was yoked with Corpus Christi Church. Sacred Heart celebrated its first 100 years of parish life with a Mass on September 7, 1997.

ST. GABRIEL, WINDSOR

Established 1894
Current Pastor: Father Richard J. Neumann
Parochial Vicar: Father Robert J. Grant
1100 households

From 1852 to 1892, the section of Windsor now encompassed by St. Gabriel parish was the responsibility of St. Mary, Windsor Locks. In 1853, Father James Smyth offered the area's first Mass at the home of John Hickey. On November 1, 1865, Father Smyth purchased an Episcopal church named for St. Gabriel, a small frame structure directly north behind the present day church on Windsor Avenue. In 1892, St. Gabriel passed to the jurisdiction of St. Joseph parish, Poquonock. On May 16, 1915, the cornerstone of a new St. Gabriel was blessed by St. Joseph pastor Father John J. Fitzgerald. On May 14, 1916, Bishop John J. Nilan dedicated the church. The prelate raised St. Gabriel to parish status in 1921. Father John F. Quinn was appointed first residing pastor. In the spring of 1956 Father Quinn bought three former public school buildings on Bloomfield Avenue from the Town of Windsor. In September 1956, St. Gabriel School opened in the purchased buildings staffed by the Felician Sisters. In 1985, the Felician Sisters left the parish and were succeeded by the Sisters of St. Joseph.

St. Gabriel Church

ST. GERTRUDE, WINDSOR

Established 1947
Current Pastor: Father Maurice J. Barry
400 households

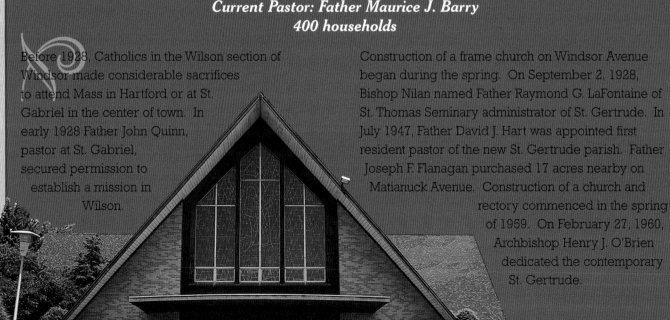

Before 1928, Catholics in the Wilson section of Windsor made considerable sacrifices to attend Mass in Hartford or at St. Gabriel in the center of town. In early 1928 Father John Quinn, pastor at St. Gabriel, secured permission to establish a mission in Wilson.

Construction of a frame church on Windsor Avenue began during the spring. On September 2, 1928, Bishop Nilan named Father Raymond G. LaFontaine of St. Thomas Seminary administrator of St. Gertrude. In July 1947, Father David J. Hart was appointed first resident pastor of the new St. Gertrude parish. Father Joseph F. Flanagan purchased 17 acres nearby on Matianuck Avenue. Construction of a church and rectory commenced in the spring of 1959. On February 27, 1960, Archbishop Henry J. O'Brien dedicated the contemporary St. Gertrude.

St. Mary, Windsor Locks

Established 1852
Current Pastor: Father Robert A. O'Grady
Parochial Vicar: Father Francis P. McDonnell
1600 households

Irish workers along the Enfield Falls canal attended the first area Mass in August 1827 when Father John Power, Vicar General of New York, arrived for a sick call. From 1829 to 1852, priests from Hartford traveled to Windsor Locks. Though Father Hugh Carmody was officially appointed on February 9, 1852, to serve the Windsor Locks vicinity, the organized church really began with the labors of Father James Smyth, who was named resident pastor on June 24. Father Smyth purchased land and broke ground for a church on August 17, 1852. Bishop Bernard O'Reilly blessed the cornerstone on September 14. The first Mass was celebrated in the new church on March 27, 1853, and later dedicated that year. The immediate concerns for religious education resulted in the erection of a small brick school in 1865. On January 2, 1866, the school opened to 100 pupils taught by lay persons. A new school building was dedicated on August 11, 1889, and staffed by the Sisters of St. Joseph, Springfield Province. In 1908, the Sisters of St. Joseph of Chambery replaced the Springfield Josephites. When the Sisters of St. Joseph departed in 1972, the parish school closed. The July 1991 installation Mass of Father William J. Hilliard was the last public appearance by Archbishop John F. Whealon before his death in 1991.

ST. ROBERT BELLARMINE, WINDSOR LOCKS

Established 1962
Current Pastor: Father Thomas F. Farrell
500 households

When St. Robert Bellarmine was established, historic St. Mary parish in Windsor Locks had ministered to Catholics of the town for more than a century. A modern mission church was erected in the southwest section of the town in 1960 under Father August Finnance of the mother parish. Created by Archbishop Henry J. O'Brien on September 2, 1962, the new parish of St. Robert Bellarmine became the first Catholic enclave in Windsor Locks taken from the expansive jurisdiction of the town's mother parish. On September 22, Father Leonard T. Goode, the first resident pastor, arrived and resided at St. Mary. In 1963, the pastor purchased the property of a local Italian group, the St. Oronzo Society, and transformed it into the Bellarmine Center. In 1965, another two acres of land adjacent to the church was secured as the site of a rectory constructed under Father Goode's direction.

ST. JOSEPH, WINSTED

Established 1853
Current Pastor: Father Bruce Czapla, O.F.M.
Parochial Vicar:
Father Albert McMahon, O.F.M.
1200 households

Catholic residents in Winsted, or Clifton, as it was once called, were initially the responsibility of Hartford and New Haven priests. The first Catholic Mass in town was celebrated by Father James Lynch at the west district schoolhouse for about 40 Catholics. On November 1, 1847, Waterbury's Father Michael O'Neil assumed responsibility for Winsted. When on March 31, 1851, Father Thomas Quinn was assigned to the Norfolk mission, he officially began ministering to Winsted. The new pastor gathered his congregation for Mass at Camp's Hall. The cornerstone was ready for blessing in 1853 and the dedication followed in February 1854. On January 1, 1865, Bishop Francis P. McFarland consigned the parish to the care of the Franciscan Fathers of New York under Father Leo Rizzo da Saracena, O.F.M., as pastor. It has continued to be the responsibility of the Holy Name province and subsequently the Immaculate Conception Province of the Franciscan Order. The dynamic friar opened a parochial school in the church basement on August 15, 1865, staffed by Franciscan Sisters from Allegany, New York. A monastery for the friars was constructed in 1866 and in 1887, St. Anthony School was built. The cornerstone of a new Gothic church was blessed on August 30, 1914 and dedicated on July 16, 1916. The former church was converted into a parish hall. On October 3, 1964, modern St. Anthony School was dedicated.

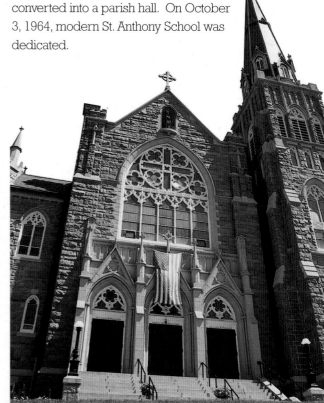

St. Maria Goretti, Wolcott

Established 1973
Current Pastor: Father William R. Sokolowski
800 households

St. Maria Goretti began as a mission of St. Pius X, established by Archbishop John F. Whealon on June 24, 1971, to serve the northeast section of Wolcott. First Masses were celebrated on July 31 and August 1 by newly appointed mission pastor Father Gerald C. Mullins. The Alcott School had been made available for Sunday liturgy by the local Board of Education. For daily Mass, the Knights of Columbus building was used. In January 1972, St. Maria Goretti became the patron of the mission. St. Maria Goretti was designated a full parish on September 8, 1973. In March 1974, about 10 acres on Woodtick Road were purchased from the New Britain Water Department as a church site. After a Mass at the rectory chapel, ground was broken on May 6, 1975, in the presence of 100 parishioners. Archbishop Whealon dedicated the brick colonial style church on November 9, 1975. A spacious social hall adjoined the church.

St. Pius X, Wolcott

Established 1955
Current Pastor: Father Henry A. Balchunas
1700 households

Wolcott Catholics attended Sacred Heart and SS. Peter and Paul parishes in Waterbury before Archbishop Henry J. O'Brien officially established St. Pius X parish on January 7, 1956. Actually, founding pastor Father Raymond P. Shea had been appointed in the spring of 1955, but the disastrous statewide flood in August delayed the work of establishing the new parish. A tract of land for the new church had been obtained from the Scovill Manufacturing Company in 1955. Father Shea celebrated the first two parish Masses in the auditorium of the Frisbie School on January 8, 1956. Father Shea purchased a home on Woodtick Road on January 13, 1956, and on February 10 he offered a Mass of Thanksgiving in its basement chapel. Father Shea broke ground on October 21, 1956. Finally, on November 24, 1957, the new St. Pius X church was dedicated. The parish grew so steadily that in January 1971 a mission, named after St. Maria Goretti, was designated in the northeast portion of St. Pius' territory. It would later be given full parish status.

CHURCH OF THE ASSUMPTION, WOODBRIDGE

Established 1924
Current Pastor: Father Gene E. Gianelli
Parochial Vicar: Father Alphonso Fontana
1300 households

Irish Catholic immigrants in early 19th century Woodbridge were visited by New Haven priests, including Father James McDermott. While other Woodbridge Catholics attended St. Aedan Church, Italian immigrants were sustained in faith by regular affiliation with New Haven's and Hamden's Italian national parishes. The initiative to establish a mission in Woodbridge emerged from the prayerful efforts of the St. Ann Rosary Society. The Italian families of Woodbridge met regularly at the Warner School. Bishop John J. Nilan created the Assumption mission of St. Ann parish, Hamden, in 1924. The Perrotti family soon donated land on the Litchfield Turnpike and the entire immigrant community volunteered labor and funds to build a church. Only a basement chapel at first, the Church of the Assumption was dedicated in November 1924 by St. Ann's Father Alvaro Santolini. The upper church was finally completed and dedicated on March 30, 1952. Growth of the Catholic population of the area resulted in Archbishop O'Brien's making

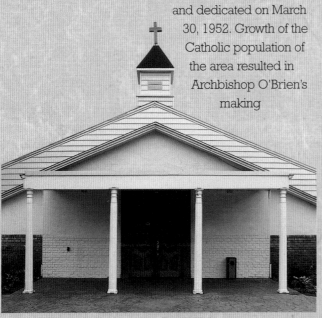

Assumption Church a parish on October 17, 1957, with Father John A. Horgan appointed first pastor. A suburban population explosion soon required a bigger church. At this point the town of Bethany was added to Assumption parish. Construction began, and Archbishop O'Brien dedicated the new contemporary style Assumption Church and hall on December 23, 1962.

ST. TERESA, WOODBURY

Established 1903
Current Pastor: Father Robert M. Kwiatkowski
1200 households

There were a few Catholics in Woodbury by 1850. Masses were celebrated periodically at private homes and later at the town hall. During these formative years, Woodbury was subject to various ecclesiastical jurisdictions that included Waterbury until 1855, Derby until 1859, Waterbury again until 1866, Naugatuck until 1873, New Milford until 1885, Seymour until 1886, and finally Watertown until 1916. At a cost of $10,400, Father John Loftus, pastor of Watertown, built a handsome mission church in Woodbury. The cornerstone was blessed on June 30, 1903, and the dedication was held on September 4, 1904. The combined Woodbury-Middlebury area was subsequently established as a parish on March 1, 1916, with Father William Judge appointed resident pastor. After assuming the pastorate at St. Teresa, Father Eugene P. Cryne resolved in September 1922 that the parochial seat be moved to Middlebury, where the majority of the congregation resided. St. Teresa thus reverted to mission status. In 1955, altered population patterns required, once again, a resident pastor in Woodbury. Father Francis P. Barrett was appointed to that ministry.

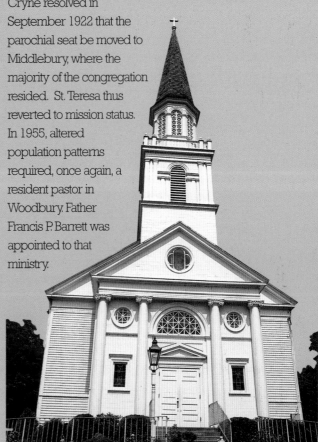

St. Agnes, Woodmont

Established 1906
Current Pastor: Father Francis X. Callahan
500 households

Catholics of Woodmont were the responsibility of Milford pastors during the early 20th century. A chapel, initially to be named for the Sacred Heart, was erected by the pastor of St. Mary, Milford, in 1906. Around this time the name of the mission was changed to St. Agnes. With a hefty Catholic population center now concentrated in Woodmont, Archbishop Henry J. O'Brien raised St. Agnes from mission to parish status on July 8, 1954, with Father John R. O'Connor appointed first pastor. The vacant Woodmont Country Club building was purchased for $1800. Parishioners donated their own labor to refit the edifice as a parish hall. The following year, the parish decided to build a new church. Upon completion, the new church was dedicated in May 1960.

Our Lady of Fatima, Yalesville

Established 1956
Current Pastor: Father Salvatore F. Cavagnuolo
2100 households

On January 17, 1954, Archbishop Henry J. O'Brien established a mission in Yalesville under Father Eugene Moriarty, pastor of Holy Angels Church, South Meriden. Originally to be named for the Blessed Sacrament, the Yalesville mission was placed under the patronage of Our Lady of Fatima at Archbishop O'Brien's suggestion. Father Moriarty celebrated mission Masses at the Yalesville School starting on January 31, 1954. Ground was broken for the new church on July 12, 1955, on land donated by Mr. and Mrs. Joseph McNally on Hope Hill Road. A Spanish style church was completed and dedicated on August 18, 1956, by Archbishop O'Brien. In September 1960, full parish status was conferred, and Father Edwin A. O'Brien was appointed first resident pastor.

Do not be afraid, for I am with you;
Do not be afraid, for I am your God.

Is. 40:10

FURTHER RESOURCES

For a more detailed background of the history of the Archdiocese of Hartford, researchers should consult the following sources, all available at the Archives:

PRIMARY SOURCES:

Deceased Priest Personnel Files, 1880 – present
Files generated by the Chancery. Includes photographs, list of assignments, correspondence, and newspaper clippings. Organized alphabetically by surname.

Kearney Notes, by Msgr. William Kearney, early 1960's
Msgr. Kearney compiled research notes on each parish in the diocese with the intent of writing a more accurate history of the archdiocese. Includes histories of parishes in the dioceses of Hartford, Bridgeport, and Norwich.

Parish Annual Reports, 1851-present
Reports contain information on many aspects of parish life: financial reports, parish statistics, signatures of trustees and pastors, etc. Provides a useful profile of a parish. A finding aid is available.

Parish Boundary Lines
Includes itemized list of streets dividing one parish from another. Some may include maps of parish area.

Parish Correspondence Files
Consists of correspondence between a parish and the Chancery. Also includes newspaper clippings relating to the parish supplied by the archives. Organized alphabetically by town and then by parish.

Parish Deeds, 1833-present
Includes warranty and quitclaim deeds for most churches in the archdiocese.
Arranged alphabetically by town and then by parish.

Parish Histories
Consists of histories and programs produced by a parish for an anniversary or
other celebration. Organized alphabetically by town and then by parish. Not
all parishes are represented in this collection. A finding aid is available.

NOTE: Access Restrictions may apply to any of the Collections.

SECONDARY SOURCES:

The Catholic Transcript, 1829 – present
Archdiocesan newspaper, available on microfilm (not indexed).

The Catholic Church in Connecticut, by Thomas S. Duggan, 1930
Useful overall history of Catholicism in our state.

Connecticut Catholic Directory, 1954 – present
Directory of parishes and archdiocesan agencies. Includes parish
establishment dates.

Hartford's Catholic Legacy: Leadership,
by Sister Dolores Liptak, RSM, 2000
Thorough treatment of the biographies of the various bishops and archbishops
of Hartford since its founding as a diocese in 1843. Written by a former
archivist and historian of the Archdiocese of Hartford.

Hartford's Catholic Legacy: Parishes, by Joseph Duffy, 1994
Recent work published for the 150th anniversary of the Archdiocese of
Hartford. Includes succinct histories of each parish in the archdiocese.

The History of the Catholic Church in the New England States, 2v., by
Very Rev. William Byrne, D.D., 1899.
Volume I focuses on the Archdiocese of Boston, and the dioceses of
Providence, Portland, and Manchester. Volume II focuses on the dioceses of
Hartford, Burlington, and Springfield. James O'Donnell submitted his
History of the Diocese of Hartford to be included in this volume.

History of the Diocese of Hartford, by James O'Donnell, 1900
Gives an overview of the history of the diocese and includes parish histories
and photographs. This work is also included in the *History of the Catholic
Church in the United States*, Volume 2, by William Byrne and published in
1899.

Official Catholic Directory 1833 – present.
Directory of dioceses in the United States, Mexico and Canada.
Arranged alphabetically by diocese.